Anat Levit is an Israeli poet and au
has published eleven books and
prestigious awards for her works
the Wertheim Prize for Poetry, the
Prize for Literary Criticism, and tl
Minister's Prize for Hebrew Literar

Yardenne Greenspan is a writer and Hebrew
translator. Her translations have been pub-
lished by Restless Books, St. Martin's Press,
Akashic and Farrar, Straus & Giroux. She is a
regular contributor to *Ploughshares*.

Seven Cats I Have Loved

ANAT LEVIT

Translated from the Hebrew by
Yardenne Greenspan

This paperback edition published 2023

First published in Great Britain in 2022 by
Serpent's Tail,
an imprint of Profile Books Ltd
29 Cloth Fair
London EC1A 7JQ
www.serpentstail.com

1 3 5 7 9 10 8 6 4 2

Typeset in Freight Text by MacGuru Ltd
Printed and bound in Great Britain by
CPI Group (UK) Ltd, Croydon CRO 4YY

A CIP catalogue record for this book is
available from the British Library.

ISBN 978 1 80081 270 3
eISBN 978 1 80081 271 0

MIX
Paper | Supporting
responsible forestry
FSC® C171272
FSC
www.fsc.org

For that which befalleth the sons of men befalleth beasts; even one thing befalleth them: as the one dieth, so dieth the other; yea, they have all one breath; so that a man hath no preeminence above a beast: for all is vanity.

Ecclesiastes 3:19

Contents

The Beginning // 1

Falling from a Great Height // 4

If We Were Cats // 11

A Fateful Decision // 18

A Dawnless Night // 23

Can a Cat Change Its Fur? // 31

Cleo or Cleopatra // 42

About Love, and the Love of Food // 50

A Gateway to Stray Cats // 57

The Soul of an Utter Saint // 66

Sweetheart's Lesson // 81

What Is Love? // 91

A Prince in Disguise // 98

An End Without an End // 116

A New Chapter // 130

Acknowledgements // 133

The Beginning

The Beginning

Just a few weeks after my first cat came to live with me, it occurred to me that, if one were able to choose one's children according to how well suited their personalities were to our parental skills, I would have been fortunate to grant myself children as easy-going as my cat.

Her intense blue eyes gazed at me sagely. Her shorn grey-brown coat was silky to the touch. She taught herself to use the litterbox on her first day in my home, leaving me marvelling at her cleverness as the soft padding of her paws on the floor imbued the space with a sense of tranquillity.

She came to us mere months after my divorce. My daughters, Daphna and Shlomit, asked me to bring home a pet. At first, I purchased a white puppy as compensation for the absence of their father. But in a matter of days, I discovered that the dog's demeanour did not match the name I'd picked out for her. Squeals of terror sounded regularly, as Lady pounced onto the four- and six-year-old girls' beds, licking their faces. Not a week went by before they demanded that I return Lady to the pet store and bring back a cat instead. I didn't try too hard to convince them to give the dog a chance, because, in truth, she was a burden for me as well. I walked her three times a day, and spent the time in between walks cleaning up her messes from every room of the apartment. But in spite of it all, I did feel a spark of affection for Lady. I hastened our separation in order to prevent myself from becoming inextricably attached to her.

Lady the dog was replaced with a cat. Until that time, I had no special affinity for cats, but I'd heard people say that caring for cats was an undemanding endeavour. The litterbox excuses one from the obligation to walk the cat morning, noon and night, in all kinds of weather, for the rest of the animal's life. I also heard that house cats sleep for many hours of the day and do not require much attention during their waking hours.

Shelly, my first cat, was perfectly suited for my limited animal-rearing skills. I named her in honour of a beloved friend who had passed away just a few months earlier.

During Shelly's first weeks in our home, I still could not have guessed that within the course of one year she would topple all of my previous reservations about sharing my home with an animal. That same year, she was joined by four other kittens whose tiny eyes, pleading with me from the small cages at the pet store, melted my heart and bound me to them with the chains of fate.

I named them Afro, Lady, Mocha and Jesse.

If love is real, I have been lucky enough to experience it thanks to the presence of these cats in my life, sharing it intimately for years on end, without the barriers of skin and fur.

Falling from a Great Height

In the very first year of their lives, three of my cats must have been eager to test the human falsehood regarding cats' ability to fall from a great height and land safely on their feet. Afro, Mocha and Lady behaved like oblivious children; they accidentally slipped off the stone wall of my rooftop terrace. Even after this initiation ceremony, all of my cats continued to enjoy the roof at all hours of the day and night. They liked to slip out through the living-room window and onto the roof for a breath of fresh air.

For the most part, house cats only face the outside world when they are ill. Then they are imprisoned in a small plastic carrier and hauled over to the vet's clinic as they yowl their distress.

*

I would make the rounds several times a day, peeking into each room to make sure that all of the cats were pleasantly ensconced – sleeping or dozing off with eyes half open. Whenever one of them was unaccounted for I would become restless and embark on a search of every regular hiding place: underneath the beds or the covers, behind the piano, or inside one of the wardrobes which the cats used their front paws to open.

This was the case on the morning when I discovered that Jesse had gone missing. After a quick look through the apartment, I began to call his name loudly. A few moments later, I heard a distant, fractured meowing. Bolstered, I continued to call out Jesse's name so that he would keep yowling at me; he sounded like he was trapped and crying for help.

Finally, I found the cat stuck behind the fridge. He'd made it in but couldn't make it out. I quickly pushed the fridge away from the wall, picked up Jesse in my arms, and kissed him, trying to reassure both of us. I had no idea if he'd only slipped behind the fridge that morning or if, God forbid, he'd spent the entire night back there. I knew I would never be able to answer that question, and took solace in the notion that perhaps cats knew how to skip from one event to the next without carrying the burden of human memory, which accumulated unhappy experiences.

Indeed, a few minutes later, Jesse returned to prowling the apartment with his usual ease, as if no serious trauma had befallen him.

Whenever the daily roll-call found one of the cats missing in action, I would rush down to the yard to search for him or her in the area right below the roof. Having called out their names, I would hunt down Afro, Lady or Mocha – hiding, frightened, behind one of the building's gas tanks.

A careful examination of the fall victim's body always proved that they hadn't landed on their feet. Each one was in shock at the fall – a four-storey drop into an unknown abyss; and I could see in them an innate fear of other, unknown cats, any one of which might choose to attack their own brethren in that moment of vulnerability.

My three furry paratroopers did not flinch when I hovered over them, speaking words of compassion. Then I carried them home, their eyes fixed on my face, revealing terrible misery. I would bring them to the vet the very same day, hoping against hope that this time they wouldn't require a cast to fix broken legs.

In the days that followed, I would observe the injured cats with amused curiosity, watching as they attempted to remove the burdensome bandage with one of their healthy legs. Like an accident victim who must learn to deal with an unexpected impairment, my bandaged cats soon discovered their skill for limping on three legs.

Afro fell off the roof twice. The second event threatened to end one of my own, human, romantic relationships. One day, my boyfriend and I had plans to take a trip to the Cave of the Patriarchs. He'd often accused me of loving my cats more than I loved him. I denied the allegation, of course. That day, I had a brutal test of love to pass.

I woke up early that morning, wanting to be ready to go when my boyfriend came to pick me up. But then I was startled to find Afro gone. I called his name over and over again, frantically scouring every hiding place, including the roof. The appointed pick-up time grew nearer, and my dual anxiety exacerbated: I couldn't leave home without knowing where Afro was, but I couldn't disappoint my boyfriend, either.

I hurried down to the street and circled the building once, twice, three times. Each footstep was accompanied with a prayer that Afro would be found soon – perhaps even in one piece. I kept calling his name until I finally gave up and went back upstairs. In a wary voice, I informed my boyfriend over the phone that Afro was gone. To my surprise, he tried to reassure me. With full confidence, he promised me that when I came home that evening I would find Afro in one of the bedrooms, entirely indifferent to the racket I'd raised over him that morning.

Until that day, I had never left home without knowing that all of my cats were safe and sound, lying on the floor tiles or on the beds. That day – which we'd planned and looked forward to a long time in advance – I had to make a swift choice between my two-legged boyfriend, whom I loved and whom I feared might leave me in a huff over the disruption of our romantic adventure – over a cat, no less! – and between my four-legged companion whom I loved just as much.

The decision sliced through my heart.

I ended up going on the trip, but throughout the day I kept glancing at my watch, wishing the trip over so I could return home and find out what had really happened to Afro. When we arrived at the Cave of the Patriarchs, I asked to be alone with my thoughts in soulful solitude, so I could say a prayer for Afro's safe return.

That afternoon, as my boyfriend and I started making our way home, my phone rang. My prayers had been answered! My neighbour, Rachel, who had her own cat and dog, called to inform me that during their daily walk, her dog tugged on his leash, pulling her into the yard adjacent to our building. There, hiding in a thick bush, was a frightened Afro.

I asked Rachel to take Afro to the vet's clinic, and rushed over there to meet them. I petted him for a long time, my eyes welling up with guilt, regret and joy. Then I brought him home, temporarily limping, with a red cut on his lower lip. This time, no cast was necessary.

Over the next few days, I wondered what

would have happened to Afro had the dog's powerful nose not detected him. Along with the pain of picturing my cat hiding in a bush for an entire day, injured, abandoned and terrified, I held on to the comfort of knowing that without the help of the curious dog, Afro and I would have had a horrifying night to endure – torn apart, with no idea of how physically close we really were.

Life with cats often resembles a game of hide-and-seek, but without any of the pleasure.

If We Were Cats

Daphna and Shlomit took offence whenever I referred to the cats as 'my children'. They made it clear that cats could not be considered their equals, and that my own flesh and blood ought to be superior to any other living being. They, and only they, were the fruits of my loins.

Usually, I offered a quick apology and corrected the slip of the tongue that had erroneously distorted the hierarchy of creation. But deep in my heart, I knew I couldn't really tell my feelings for my daughters apart from my feelings for my cats.

Sometimes I even secretly accused myself of discriminating against Daphna and Shlomit and in favour of the cats. I knew the reason lay in the fact that I didn't have as many expectations of the cats as I had of my daughters, who often failed to meet them. I was often aggravated at my daughters for ignoring my need for a tidy home and leaving their clothes, shoes, games and books scattered in every room. I was blatantly furious whenever they stained the floor with mud or food crumbs, and gave them a loud piece of my mind when they ruined an electrical appliance or unintentionally damaged a knick-knack or a piece of furniture.

On the other hand, when Mocha or Jesse vomited on the floor or the rugs after having ripped off and chewed up leaves from the plants, I never even told them off. As I cleaned up the ugly stains, I reminded myself that the cats had to eat leaves and vomit in order to clear out their digestive systems, which occasionally got clogged by furballs. I wasn't angry when Afro destroyed the couches and chairs for the purpose of sharpening his claws, even after I bought him a special scratching post. I was upset about the damaged furniture, but took comfort in the knowledge that it wasn't valuable, and that now I had an excuse to update the living room.

The main reason I gave my cats the benefit of the doubt was that I knew they were untrainable. This inborn feature often aroused my envy; I longed to be more like them. I found that I inflicted pain upon myself by virtue of being trained almost from birth to please and fulfil the needs of my beloveds. I yearned to make them happy, even at the price of the extinction of my own happiness.

Surprisingly, my misgivings about my treatment of Daphna and Shlomit reached an apex because of Shelly, whose habits didn't typically cause any disruption. She spent most of her days sprawled over the long wooden shelf that hung above the living-room couch. The shelf was covered with small plants, books and figurines, and Shelly would hop lightly between the couch and the shelf, never disturbing any of the objects on it. When her eyes weren't closed, the shelf served as her observation post.

She was there almost every hour of the day, except for twice a week, when I used the vacuum cleaner. The commotion frightened Shelly, driving her into one of the other rooms.

But one day, she chose to nap on a different shelf, where my state-of-the-art stereo system was set up. She was napping there, and I had momentarily forgotten about her vacuum sensitivity and turned it on. The cat jumped to the floor, and the stereo system followed suit.

With great trepidation, I turned off the vacuum and returned the system to its place. I was convinced it was broken. I turned on the radio, and when the sounds of classical music emerged I was filled with joy, but also with sadness for having frightened Shelly. I went looking for her in order to apologise and reassure her, but was then pricked with an intense guilt towards Daphna and Shlomit. I knew that if one of the girls had knocked over the expensive stereo system, face clouding with horror at my attack of rage, I would feel none of the compassion that Shelly brought out of me so effortlessly. As I rubbed the cat's fur, I vowed to learn how to produce more of that same forgiveness towards my daughters.

Sometimes, I worried that even the health of my daughters mattered to me less than the health of my cats. When one of them complained that she wasn't feeling well, I never rushed her to the doctor, relying instead on the healing powers of time. But at the mere suspicion of a disruption to the health of one of the cats I would rush them to the vet, gripped with terror over their impending death.

This is what I did whenever Lady hid in the wardrobe for longer than usual, or when Mocha fasted for hours at a time, refusing even his favourite cold cuts, or when Afro woke up in the morning with an eye veiled with yellow mucus.

In response to my guilt over neglecting my daughters, who were fully capable of expressing their distress at times of illness through words and tears, I convinced myself that mute, restrained misery simply inspired greater compassion and concern in me.

There was something else that contributed to my inner turmoil regarding my status as main caretaker of my daughters' and cats' well-being: even when Daphna and Shlomit were just babies, I had no qualms about being away from home for days or even weeks at a time. I'd travel with their father, replenishing my parenting energies. But I never dreamed of leaving my cats alone at home for more than a few hours.

One day, when Daphna, Shlomit and I went

on a day trip, I was plagued with longing and concern for the cats I'd left at home. I called home twice, waiting for the answering machine on my desk to pick up, then spoke into the recording device. I called each cat by their name and reassured them with loving words. In my mind's eye, I saw all five cats gathering round, listening. I wanted to calm their nerves, to assure them I was with them in spirit, if not in person.

The truth was, I never left Daphna and Shlomit alone at home until they were teenagers. When I did, I found replacement mothers for them, such as grandmothers or babysitters. I often called the girls. Their detailed descriptions over the phone, informing me of the pleasures they experienced while I was gone, taught me that my daughters never suffered from my absence.

The final 'discriminatory' issue stemmed from my dwindling finances, a problem that troubled me now and then. When this happened, I would summon the girls for a family meeting, pleading with them to avoid unnecessary purchases, but never even considered eliminating the cats' deluxe feeding habits. I knew I wouldn't be able to explain to them why I had to temporarily interrupt their high-quality diet. I was also worried that switching their foods would cause them to stop eating altogether.

While I often agonised over being a failed and failing mother to Daphna and Shlomit, I yearned to come back in my next life as a cat so that I could live in the kind of home I always tried to give my furry children.

A Fateful Decision

If Shelly could speak rather than only communicate with her eyes, and I'd asked her at three months old if she would ever want to have kittens, she would likely have said, 'There's nothing I want more in this world than to become a mother.'

I'll never forgive myself for my automatic decision to sterilise her. I had enough on my plate raising Daphna and Shlomit, which I did almost entirely by myself after my divorce. Having bought four additional kittens of my own, I couldn't imagine myself joyfully enduring a cat's pregnancy and delivery.

It was therefore easy to take Amos the vet's word for it when he explained that cats don't have the same conscious birthing urge as human females. That's why, he argued, preventing Shelly from having kittens wouldn't be unethical. I was also bolstered by the knowledge that sterilising Shelly would grant her a longer and healthier life than a cat whose God-given female body was not subject to human interventions.

I therefore rushed to take advantage of the control I had over my first cat's life. Without a thought to the cruelty involved in ignoring her own needs and desires, I sentenced her to a life of childlessness.

Three events that resulted from Shelly's sterilisation brought on intense reservations. The first took place at the end of the day she was sterilised, and worried me no end.

On Friday morning, I left Shelly at the clinic without informing her that her little body was about to undergo major surgery. Amos the vet promised me that the surgery was simple, that Shelly would be sedated and returned to me shortly after the operation was over. He didn't anticipate any complications during the procedure or any difficulties in coming out of anaesthesia.

By noon, Shelly was back home, sound asleep on the rug in my bedroom. The hours ticked by and Shabbat started, but Shelly continued to lie limply, eyes shut, in the same spot where I'd left her hours earlier. My deep concern over her lingering in sleep was coupled by my unease about calling the vet at home on the weekend. Finally, I felt compelled to pick up the phone and inform him that Shelly was still asleep.

Thirty minutes later, Amos arrived at my door, his expression troubled. I placed the sleeping cat on the bed between us so that he could listen to her heartbeat. After he found it normal, he began to nudge Shelly gently in an attempt to quicken her release from the webs of forced sleep.

We only breathed sighs of relief once we saw the cat opening her eyes and attempting to stand up. Apologetically, Amos, who had by that point become my friend, confessed that he must have injected Shelly with too much an-aesthesia. I was completely absorbed in watching Shelly falter on the floor independently, having wriggled out of my supporting arms. On trembling legs, she limped over to the litterbox I'd placed in the room for her, climbed in with effort, and dazedly relieved herself.

*

The second element that made me feel that I'd done Shelly a disservice by so frivolously preventing her from becoming a mother was her obvious affection towards the unfamiliar kittens I brought home so often. Each of them enjoyed a generous welcome from my eldest fur-baby. She never expressed any reservation or jealous aggression, the way a child suddenly forced to share their parents' attentions or their bedroom might.

Daphna, Shlomit and I watched with excitement as Shelly softly approached her adopted brothers and sisters – who may also have been her adopted kittens – and licked each of their little heads in turn.

I was also impressed with Shelly when she, Mocha, Cleo, Lady and Jesse came to the kitchen to eat together. This mostly happened in the morning. All but Shelly would lean over their full bowls, heads touching, while Shelly waited. Only after the other diners were satiated and scattered throughout the apartment would she approach the bowls and eat what they had left behind.

Shelly's caring restraint inspired deep admiration in me when I compared her to humans, who had such trouble showing generosity, especially in moments of hunger. Though I always made sure to address my daughters' hunger before taking care of my own, I often grew impatient, searching for and finding excuses to snap at them.

The atrocity of Shelly's sterilisation hit me most intensely when an aching feline yowl sounded from Daphna's room. I knew what had preceded it: Shelly had hopped onto my daughter's bed, gripped a green stuffed frog between her teeth, then jumped off the bed and dropped the replacement baby on the floor.

After she sounded that heart-breaking yowl, Shelly would leave the room, purged of her grief.

Daphna and Shlomit were the ones who dubbed Shelly 'Mama Cat', in spite of her womblessness. And I, out of pure selfishness, chose to sterilise my other cats as well.

A Dawnless Night

Shelly served as surrogate mother to four cats that she hadn't birthed, and reminded us bipeds of a four-legged queen. Her delicate gait and the tranquillity that often veiled her piercing eyes filled us with awe. I had to admit to myself that she enjoyed more attention from my daughters and myself than any of our other cats.

Soon after I learned of her death, I was struck by the thought that perhaps she chose to leave us in body so as to tear down the wall that she'd unintentionally erected between us and the other four cats.

The day after Shelly's urgent hospitalisation, when I was asked by the vet who'd treated her through the night if I wanted to bury her or have the animal hospital cremate her body, I chose cremation without a moment's hesitation. I felt that Shelly was asking me to help her become pure spirit as quickly as possible, free from the prison of the body that ruled the home she had loved so deeply ever since arriving as a kitten.

Perhaps I also didn't linger because of the shock caused by the news of her unexpected death.

Two days earlier, Shelly had appeared perfectly healthy. Then, all of a sudden, I noticed a few drops of blood next to one of the plants in the living room. After anxiously following each cat around, I discovered the source.

That afternoon, Shelly paused before me in the middle of the living room and excreted the frightening drops with obvious effort, as if to help me solve the mystery of the sick cat. I called Amos the vet right away and asked him to come see her urgently. He explained he was out of town but promised to call me later that day. He reassured me that Shelly was most likely suffering from a curable kidney disease.

But Shelly's condition only grew worse, and by the time Amos called me back, she was already curled up in a hiding place she'd made for herself between the piano and the wall. She didn't eat or drink a thing that day. I knew that a sick cat would sometimes neglect even their most basic physical needs – food and water – and arrive at the brink of death in a matter of days.

When Amos called, he apologised for not yet finding the time to come over and examine Shelly. I grew hot with silenced anger when he recommended that I bring her to the clinic, where, he promised, a colleague of his would check her thoroughly and reliably.

I asked Shlomit to accompany me. She helped me put a weak Shelly into the carrier, and we went to the clinic together. We sat in the waiting room, staring at the closed door, behind which the vet was treating a sobbing dog.

Had I given in to the panic I felt over my cat, I would have forgotten my manners at once, burst into the examination room, and demanded that Shelly be seen immediately. The restraint of this desire to the point of absolute suppression has to do with my age-old fear of being rejected by other people – especially those whose help I desperately need. In front of that closed door, I was trapped in an intense inner battle between the urge to demand a treatment that would favour Shelly over every other animal and the fear of being rebuked and inadvertently inspiring the vet's hostility towards my cat.

The entire time, Shelly lay collapsed, exhausted, on the bottom of the carrier I held on my lap. Every few moments, I gazed into her faded eyes and felt my guts twist. My cat's silent suffering ultimately pushed me to yell out her distress at the closed door, behind which the dog owner and the vet were, by this point, merely chit-chatting.

The door opened, and I was faced with the unfamiliar vet, who immediately noticed Shelly's dangling tongue and disrupted breathing. In a matter of minutes, the cat was lying on the glimmering metal table, the air just barely making its way into her lungs. After a quick examination, I was ordered to rush Shelly to the animal hospital.

The vet determined that she was in critical condition and added an apology for the long wait, but I could think of nothing besides saving my cat's life.

I asked Shlomit to come with me to the hospital and she agreed right away. I wasn't used to such an amenable attitude from her and her sister. She must have been very worried as well. Shlomit sat in the passenger seat with the carrier on her lap, while Shelly yowled meekly inside it. I drove madly through the busy streets, manoeuvring like an ambulance without a siren or flashing lights.

It was night by the time we walked into the large waiting room of the animal hospital. Shlomit, holding the carrier containing a heavily breathing Shelly, took a seat on one of the benches, while I hurried over to the receptionist to inform her of our cat's emergency.

Minutes later, a young veterinarian with an angelic demeanour appeared before us. She peeked into the carrier and asked some questions about the brief history of Shelly's transformation from a healthy pet to a sick animal fighting for every breath. Finally, she recommended that Shelly be admitted and stay the night.

I had one more decision to make: whether to leave eleven-year-old Daphna and nine-year-old Shlomit home alone and spend the night at the hospital with Shelly so that she didn't have to be lonely and rely only on her unfamiliar caretakers, or go home and stay with the girls and the other cats – away from Shelly in body but close to her in spirit, my entire mind yearning for her quick recovery.

With the encouragement of the vet, whose blue eyes resembled Shelly's, I decided to go home and return to the hospital early the next morning. This required me to trust the vet to take devoted care of my beloved cat and keep her promise to call me with an update every few hours.

In spite of my famous anxiety about the death lurking for my cats with every slight illness, I never imagined that within a few hours I'd learn that the moment I left my cat in the hospital was to be my final goodbye to her body, whose fur my fingers had grown to know and love over the past five years.

My last words to her were a promise to return the next day and take her home.

I couldn't sleep that night. I was on alert, waiting for the vet's call. Twice I gave in to my nerves and called her, and both times she told me that there was no improvement in Shelly's condition. Two other times she called me, possibly sensing my need to hear her voice, the only mediator between me and my cat. The second time she called, just before dawn, she recommended that I get some rest, and promised to do whatever she could to make sure Shelly didn't suffer.

The next morning, after a few hours of broken sleep, I was woken up by the ringing of the phone. The vet's morose voice announced that Shelly would not be returning to me.

To this day, I still don't know the medical reason for Shelly's sudden death at such a young age. The vet told me that during the final night of my wonderful cat's life – she referred to her that way because of her submissive surrendering to all the examinations and treatments her aching body endured – no serious problems were found. And yet her grip on life had weakened at an unstoppable speed.

A week later, I returned to the animal hospital on my own to pay the cost of the failed attempts to save Shelly's life, and of her cremation.

I came home that day with an empty carrier.

I didn't mourn Shelly. For months, I kept seeing visions of her in her regular spots around the apartment – napping on Daphna's bed or the living-room couch, or watching me from the wooden shelf where she used to perch with a calmness that imbued me with a sense of peace as well.

The stuffed frog, which must have acted as a stand-in for the kitten Shelly never had, remains at the head of my bed to this day.

Can a Cat Change Its Fur?

When Daphna and Shlomit wanted a dog, then begged me to replace her with a cat, I only agreed because of the dissolution of our family that had been forced upon them. I walked into the pet store at the end of my street like a woman looking to buy a piece of clothing, jewellery or furniture. I did not understand, in those days, that animals were not commodities; that the cat I was about to purchase was a living creature who would captivate my heart, filling it with a vitality more immense than I could ever have imagined.

Of all the kittens crowding into the large cages – sleeping or wedging their noses between the bars like prisoners – my gaze fell on Shelly. With her powder-blue eyes and her grey-brown coat, she was the prettiest of them all. Though I was entirely ignorant when it came to cat classification, I guessed she belonged to some privileged breed. When I asked Jackie, the store owner, he dropped the word 'Balinese' and explained that she came with a pedigree certificate and was priced accordingly.

I took one more look at the gorgeous kitten, received my daughters' blessing, and announced to Jackie that the Balinese kitten would be ours.

I didn't know at the time that each cat's fur concealed their special nature, which was revealed only to those who sought their intimacy.

From Shelly's early days in our home, I noticed how perfectly suited she was to a shared living space. She didn't disrupt our regular routine. She slept for most hours of the day, and when she was awake she padded through the apartment with an atmospheric peacefulness. Easy baby that she was, she allowed Daphna and Shlomit to hold her in their arms, gave in to their petting, and never complained when she was put back down. She didn't move objects around, and didn't diminish the cleanliness of the apartment.

These qualities inspired me to surround

myself with four additional cats within a single year. Whenever I visited the pet store to replenish our stock of food and kitty litter, my eyes were drawn to the cats. Never to the goldfish, rabbits, hamsters, birds or dogs that filled the store. Four more times, I was captivated by the beauty of a kitten, and like a woman obsessed with building up her wardrobe, I left the store carrying Afro, Lady, Mocha and Jesse. All Persians, all as fetching as Shelly.

Afro was the second kitten I bought. After I purchased Jesse – the fifth cat – Jackie warned me that he would bar me from returning to his store. He claimed that my compulsion to buy more and more kittens was putting me in financial jeopardy and hurting the selection he wanted to offer at the store. But it wasn't because of this warning that I put a stop to my cat acquisition. It was for Daphna and Shlomit's sake. Concerned, they kept saying I must have lost my mind, and reminded me over and over again that they'd asked me to get *a* cat, not five cats that would turn our home into a menagerie.

I named Afro – a play on the Hebrew word *afor*, meaning grey – because of the colour of his fur.

His glimmering yellow eyes had charmed me at the store. His presence was also near imperceptible from the start. But unlike Shelly, his introversion was obvious. He barely looked around, and whenever we wanted to pet him, he drew his tiny claws to scratch us.

He remained aloof even after I brought Lady, Mocha and Jesse home. He avoided getting close to them, but showed no objection to their invading his territory, either. I took solace in that.

And so Afro lived among us – but not exactly with us – for five years. I believed this was his nature and that there was no reason to try to change him.

Afro began to show a new face in the months following Shelly's death, as if he was emerging from the shadow of her presence. As if she'd cleared space for him as ruler and supervisor. In those days, Afro's eyes opened to Daphna, Shlomit and me. He grew alert to our facial expressions, and seemed to stand more erect, until he appeared taller than all the other cats.

Shlomit was the first one to spot the change. She noticed that whenever the door to her room was ajar, he pushed it open with his front paw and landed on four paws right next to the chair where she was sitting and studying. He also allowed her to pet him as she did her homework. Their friendship intensified so much that when she lay awake in bed at night suffering with insomnia, she would call Afro's name and he would come right in and hop onto the bed. Then he would wait for Shlomit to stretch her arm alongside her body, and when she did so he would cling to her arm and rest his head upon it. He would lie this way as long as Shlomit held still. But when she changed her position even a little bit, he would finish his shift and leave the room.

After Shelly died, Afro slowly opened up to me. It started during lunch. When I placed a plate of beef or chicken on the table, he and Mocha would jump up together, their eyes pleading for a taste. After feeding them from my palm, wanting some space to eat as well, I would scatter bites beside my plate. When they still weren't satisfied, the two of them would break into demanding yowls, but Afro always refrained from pushing his face into my plate.

As the months went by without Shelly, Afro added my bed to the list of his favourite resting spots. He spent many a winter night lying underneath my blanket, his body flush against my warm shirt. When I took my afternoon nap, he hopped up onto the foot of the bed, stretched out beside my feet, and watched me like a loving supervisor.

Only once did I discover the wild animal concealed beneath his grey coat. One day, a bird accidentally flew into my home and landed, confused, on my bedside table. Within seconds, she was trapped between Afro's sharp teeth. She twitched with terror for long moments, trying in vain to extricate herself from the shocking death trap.

A friend who was visiting my home at the time chased the predator cat all over the apartment until he finally caught him, forced his mouth open, and allowed the bird to fly out through the window.

The most prominent feature of Afro's personality did not change from the day I brought him home and throughout the sixteen years of his life. My other cats occasionally allowed me to hold them in my arms for a brief cuddle or in order to feed them their cursed medicine. But Afro never did. Whenever I tried to pick him up off the floor he wriggled loose and strode away. When my intrusion was especially aggravating, he didn't hesitate to scratch me in retribution.

He only once allowed me to pick him up and even slip him into the carrier without resistance. This was on the day before he died. He was already suffering from an assortment of old-age maladies, and was extremely skinny underneath his grey coat, which was no longer as ravishing as it used to be.

At the beginning of that week, Afro appeared deeply fatigued. He barely ate and spent most of his time lying on the floor with his eyes closed. One morning, he suddenly jumped up on the living-room couch and sprawled out in his favourite spot. In an instant, he seemed to have recovered from all of his illnesses and regained his nearly forgotten youthful vigour. For a moment, I entertained a hope that we had many more days together to look forward to.

But the following afternoon, when I returned home after a few hours away, Afro was waiting for me at the door. When he saw me he let out a long yowl, as if he'd been awaiting my return so he could allow his bony body to collapse. He still managed to follow me into the kitchen, where he dropped onto his back. His body twisted from side to side, his legs kicking the air helplessly.

This sight filled me with pity and dread. Standing over his writhing body, I called Michael, who was my cats' regular vet at the time. He instructed me to bring Afro to the clinic at once.

I picked up the cat, who was lighter than ever, slid him into the carrier without any protest, and drove to the clinic, where we were sentenced to part for the night. Michael determined that Afro had to stay at the clinic for tests, emergency treatment and observation.

Unlike Shelly, whose life ended on her only night away from home, Afro lived through the night he was made to spend away from me. In the hours he was gone, distress twisted my insides every time I pictured my beloved cat lying alone in his time of need, locked behind the bars of the large metal cage that had replaced his home of so many years.

The next evening, when I returned to the clinic in the hopes of bringing Afro home, I found him curled up in the corner of the cage with his back turned to me. I burst into tears. I clung to the cage and spoke my great love for him with a broken voice. I begged him to come closer to the bars so I could rub his head.

Afro remained still. Michael explained that, unlike humans, who, in their time of sickness, require compassion and support, most sick cats preferred to isolate themselves. Like Afro, I too prefer solitude when I'm unwell, though I've never dared turn my back on the people who asked after my health. Afro's cold shoulder remains in my mind as a painful expression of his disdain towards me for abandoning him all night in the exile of the clinic – and in such dire health, no less.

When I asked Michael what needed to be done for the cat's recovery, he explained that Afro's condition would not allow him to go home with me, even though there was no treatment available that would spare him further misery.

The representative of the animal health industry concluded his professional advice with a single word: euthanasia. No word was more terrible to me. The decision was mine to make.

Just as I'd decided that Afro the kitten would be neutered without considering his wishes, so did I sentence him to end his life. I asked the cat longevity expert if Afro would be able to feel his life coming to an end. He promised me in a soft voice that Afro would only be put down once he was sound asleep. Then, a special substance would be injected into his body, stopping his heart. My elderly cat would float into oblivion without feeling a thing.

Without flinching from the moment when I would embrace Afro's corpse, I instructed Michael to remove him from the cage and place his emaciated body in my arms. I held him to my chest for a long moment, and with a new flood of tears thanked him for all of the years we'd spent together.

The cat looked at me motionlessly through his golden eyes. Just a few moments later, he embarked on his final journey, not knowing where he was headed and showing no signs of resistance. We had no way of returning to the life we'd shared for sixteen years.

After Michael confidently determined that

Afro's heart had stopped beating, I asked to be left alone with my dead cat. I continued hugging him, and with his eyes closed – as if he were still asleep – I gave his meagre body one final pet.

I agreed to let Afro be buried in a field outside town that was used as a pet cemetery. Since he has no tombstone, I have no way of knowing the exact whereabouts of his eternal resting place.

I refused to mourn Afro, too. For days later, I still saw him pacing through the apartment like a belatedly anointed king.

Cleo or Cleopatra

One morning, I shuffled around in a morose mood. All I wanted was to lie in bed or pace the apartment, ignoring all routine chores. The previous night, I'd received an email from a man who had excited me the very first time I'd met him, although perhaps – as had happened more than once since my divorce – I'd been led astray by my pining for any man who would fill the void that my husband had left. This new man had suddenly decided to break up with me with a handful of written words that cast a thick fog of disappointment and helplessness over me.

In the two months that had gone by since we'd met through a dating website, I'd believed we were on our way to building a relationship that would make both of us happy. The man's name was like a sign that strengthened this faith of mine. He shared his name with my father, who had died a short time earlier. I hoped that my father's fleshless hand would intervene on my behalf, fortifying my new romance.

Dazed and upset, I wandered the apartment, wallowing in the gnawing emptiness that took hold of me whenever I was forced to part from a person who had moved me, until I heard a meek meowing coming from the stairwell. At first I thought I was imagining the sound, but when it continued I started to worry that Jesse, Mocha, Lady or Afro had padded out the door when Daphna and Shlomit left for school. Perhaps one of them had slipped out without my noticing, then panicked when I slammed the front door, leaving them deserted in the stairwell.

I rushed to the door, and as soon as I opened it a smile pulled on my lips and my sorrow dissipated. A gorgeous Siamese kitten was standing on the landing. It stopped meowing right away and looked up at me with tiny blue-brown eyes that begged to be let into my home.

It looked so much like Shelly when she was a kitten. For a moment, a comforting thought passed through me – that Shelly was the one who had sent me this kitten to cheer me up.

At first I thought the Siamese was a female. Even now, after two decades of living with cats, I still have trouble telling male and female apart. The diagnosis typically entails lifting the cat's tail to check for the presence or absence of testicles. Since most cats do not easily surrender to the hands of a stranger, I avoided touching the kitten when it first walked into my home.

When the little guest began touring the apartment with a soft step and a curious demeanour, my cats remained completely indifferent. I suppose the cat's beauty was what made me assume he was a she, and so I named her Cleopatra.

In the hours that passed before Shlomit returned from school, I'd become completely enchanted by Cleopatra's gracefulness, as she wandered the apartment with liberated ease. Following her around erased all memory of the day's miserable beginnings.

When Shlomit walked in and saw our new lodger, she too fell head over heels. Without a moment's hesitation, she picked her up and petted her, and Cleopatra made no attempt to wriggle free of the embrace. The two were instantly devoted to each other.

When I asked Shlomit what we should do with the kitten, she declared that the little Siamese would stay. Just then, a knock came at the door. I opened it to find Daniel, my neighbour Rina's son. He asked if we had happened to see a Siamese kitten he'd bought as a gift for his girlfriend. The kitten, he explained, had run out of his mother's apartment that morning when she opened the door.

As Daniel spoke, Cleopatra appeared before him. He explained that she was actually a he. When he made to take the cat back, Shlomit's face fell. After Daniel left with the kitten in his arms, Shlomit begged me to go downstairs to Rina's apartment and try to convince Daniel to sell us the cat.

Since I recalled the joy the Siamese had filled my heart with just by appearing on my doorstep, I gave in to Shlomit's wishes. I went downstairs and convinced Daniel to give up Cleo – who I'd already had a chance to rename – in exchange for a generous fee.

Just as I'd done when I purchased my first cats, I reminded myself again that the large amount I'd paid would soon be forgotten and deemed meaningless compared to the happiness he would bring me every day for months and years to come.

Shlomit's face beamed when I returned upstairs with Cleo. Daphna, on the other hand, kept her distance. She'd been complaining for a while that I should have made do with Shelly, whom she'd been very attached to, and reminisced about longingly for years after she passed away. To her, Shelly was a human with an old soul – a sage of love and wisdom who'd gone up to heaven and come back down to earth in cat form.

Among other reasons, Daphna was unhappy with the number of cats in our home because of their fur, which clung to our clothes and got into our food. Shlomit also suffered from these side effects of cat-rearing, but never complained like her sister. I wasn't bothered at all by my cats' hair. In my eyes, this level of comfort was a testament to a profound love that could overcome any difficulty.

Cleo did not appear offended by Daphna's disregard. He wandered the apartment – except for Daphna's bedroom, the door of which was closed most of the time – like a young prince, displaying immense confidence to the other four cats. In spite of their seniority in our household, they seemed intimidated by him. Lady, who liked to sprawl in a position that resembled a human sitting – her back against one of the walls – would stand up on all fours whenever Cleo came near. Her little legs would then quickly carry her far away from him. Mocha – who was usually a relaxed cat, though kind of a loner – growled defensively whenever Cleo was around.

As time went by, I learned to treasure Cleo's intelligence, which was apparent first and foremost in his communicative eyes – for example, when he asked me to open a fresh tin of cat food or rub his shorn coat or clean out the litterbox that was too full of his siblings' excrement. He seemed to understand me when I addressed him, both when I spoke words of kindness and when I rebuked him for mischievous behaviour that upset the other cats.

Strangers, on the other hand, were formidable as far as he was concerned. While my other cats remained perched in place when a visitor dropped by, Cleo always scampered under one of the beds or into one of the wardrobes, revealing himself again only when the guest left. The few people who had the chance to witness him or even pet him were the ones who had a cat at home themselves. Cleo's acute sense of smell picked up on the scents of cats that had been absorbed into their owners' clothing, thus earning his trust.

One day, Cleo taught all of us just how smart and sensitive he was to his surroundings, how bold and uninhibited. That day, he decided to take his revenge against Daphna and her alienating attitude.

I was away on a trip with my daughters, and my neighbour Rachel, who had agreed to care for the cats in my absence – opening their tins of food and refilling their water bowl – called me. Flustered, she told me that Daphna's room looked as if it had been ransacked. As soon as she'd walked into the apartment she noticed that Daphna's rug was covered with bits of paper torn out of her tidy notebooks, which had been pulled off the desk. I knew immediately who the culprit was. I guessed that Daphna had left her door ajar, affording the rejected cat an opportunity for payback.

Though I feared Daphna's fury, I knew I'd better tell her about the transformation of her elegant room before we returned home, so I mustered my courage and, in an amused tone, described Cleo's pillage. As I expected, Daphna was filled with a terrible rage, accompanied by a flood of tears. But in a matter of minutes, her upset was replaced by rolling laughter that swept all of us away with it.

Cleo, my youngest cat, was the last to remain in my home. In our fourteen years together, he and I went through uplifting episodes and agonising events, all derived from the tapestry of his unique nature, which wove together great wisdom with pure malice.

About Love, and the Love of Food

From my very first year living with cats, I placed great importance on their food. People enjoy a plethora of worldly pleasures, but cats mostly gain pleasure from eating. This notion is what dictated the menu I offered them.

Just as parents these days don't need to sweat over pots of nutritious meals for their children thanks to the wide variety of prepared foods offered at grocery stores, so did I relieve myself of cooking for my cats, even when they were just kittens. From the start, they enjoyed an ongoing supply of dried food alongside different flavours of wet food, packed in small, costly tin cans. The labels on the tins specified their contents: tuna soufflé, chicken filet with aloe oil, salmon pâté, beef in sauce, shellfish, and other dishes that sounded like gourmet cooking even to a human. Many cat owners consider wet food a special treat to be offered sporadically. But for my cats, it was on the daily menu.

As soon as Shelly joined us, I arranged a little buffet area in the back of the kitchen, and it remained in place for two decades. This smorgasbord included small bowls, each containing a different flavour of wet food, along with one bowl of dry food and one bowl of water, which were replaced at least once a day.

I never imposed regular feeding hours. At any given moment, one of the cats, or all of them at once, could walk over to the buffet, sniff around, and consume an entire bowl or just have a quick bite.

I often wondered what the contents of the tins with the enticing names tasted like. But while I couldn't taste their food, my cats enjoyed both culinary worlds – the one that was exclusively theirs, and the one intended for two-legged eaters. One day, for example, I discovered that Afro and Mocha were big fans of green olives. Since that time, I left bits of olives for them on the kitchen floor, pouring a circle of juice from the tin around them.

Within seconds, the floor would be squeaky clean once more.

Occasionally Mocha, the most gluttonous of my cats, pleaded with me to treat him to cold cuts. He would cling to the fridge door, hinting at his desire for a taste of my favourite food. After he infected the other cats with the love of the sandwich meat, I often had to delay my own breakfast and spend long minutes standing by the open fridge and slipping pieces of meat into my cats' wide-open mouths.

They were especially fond of ground beef. Whenever I prepared to make meatballs for Daphna and Shlomit, I knew that minutes after I'd placed the beef on the counter, the cats would gather on the floor below me, even if just seconds earlier they had still been sound asleep in the bedrooms. They would surround me and fix me with primed looks, yearning for the moment when I tore tiny chunks off the hunk and placed them in a large plate on the floor. Then each cat would attempt to score as many pieces as possible before leaving the kitchen and resuming their naps.

Over time, I discovered that Mocha also liked fromage blanc and ice cream served to him with a spoon. Whenever he saw me eating ice cream, Jesse, who communicated with lip movements, also informed me that he would love a taste. And so I found myself faced with one of them or both of them together, offering them spoonfuls of ice cream to be licked clean.

Feeding the two cats out of spoons foreshadowed a time in their later days, when Mocha and Jesse lost their appetites. When they lost their taste for life, I'd sit on my bed, holding them in my arms as if they were babies, and try to tempt them with a bit of ice cream or white cheese. Sometimes they relented and took a tiny lick, but I was filled with deep sorrow when they gathered the remains of their strength just to turn their faces away from the spoon.

Mocha, who coveted food more than anything else, took over a corner of the kitchen counter one day and made it his own. He spent most hours of the day and night with his brown furry body fully sprawled out on the patch of counter by the sink, lying in wait to enjoy the first bite of anything I cooked. In spite of the threat of cat hair in the food, I relented, allowing him to enjoy his perch, until the yahrzeit candle that was regularly placed on the counter drove him away.

Every time I smelled scorched hair, I rushed to the kitchen to witness Mocha's tail aflame. A panicked fanning of the tail put the fire out, but I was also compelled to wrap a wet towel around it in order to cool off any charred fur.

Once, Mocha almost started a fire in our home. A thick smell of smoke summoned me into the kitchen, where I was gripped with terror at the sight of flames reaching almost all the way up to the wall cabinets. I sprayed water on the cabinets, dampening the flames that had erupted when the cat had knocked over an empty electric kettle.

Only when Mocha's legs weakened and lost their power to bounce him high up off the floor was he forced to give up his counter space. I was sorry to see the limitations of his body keeping him away from the territory that he had cherished for so many years.

Only once did I feel any concern about the fact that I overfed my cats. When Cleo was six years old, I brought him to the vet to treat an ingrown claw. As the vet tweezed it, he scolded me, remarking that he'd never seen such a fat Siamese in his life. He recommended – demanded, really – that I put Cleo on a diet. If I didn't, he threatened, I might take years off his life.

I always knew it was impossible to deny my cats food. The buffet served all the cats, and there was no way of preventing access to one of them without making his or her life miserable, which I was incapable of doing. Closing the buffet, and diminishing the lifestyle the cats had grown accustomed to, was also not an option.

The vet's recommendation to reduce Cleo's food intake reminded me of an incident that happened during Daphna's first year of life. That winter, she had trouble breathing and was admitted to the hospital, where the doctors recommended that I feed her small amounts at regular intervals so as not to overburden her system. Nevertheless, whenever Daphna cried with what I interpreted as hunger, I made her a secret bottle that she guzzled until she settled.

My cats' sense of peace was always the most important thing to me. That's why I felt there was no point in extending Cleo's life if he wouldn't be able to indulge in the food he loved so much.

As our years together went by and his body remained thick-set, I would occasionally recall the vet's warning, and thank myself in my pudgy cat's name for never having kept food from him. His cheerful appetite brought both of us joy.

In spite of his heavy weight and advanced age, Cleo continued to jump into my bed for a nap or a snuggle. He even managed to sit on my desk chair, which was higher than my bed, after a few moments of circling the chair and calculating the effort required to make the jump.

Whenever I noticed that one of the cats wasn't eating, I would panic, anticipating impending illness. The cats' love of food had a pleasing correlation to their love for me. Sometimes they would pace the kitchen, satiated, not even sniffing at the food, until I bent down to rub their backs. Then, out of the blue, they would be compelled to hurry over to the buffet and eat. I saw this as clear proof of their lust for life, which was only awakened thanks to the pleasure I offered when my hand softly and lovingly caressed their fur.

A Gateway to Stray Cats

Stray cats never received any attention from me before I met Mishely. At that point I was already raising five pedigree cats in my home. I was like a mother who had no interest in any children apart from her own – and certainly not in street urchins.

Some of the strays in my neighbourhood lived in my building's yard for years, but Mishely was the only one who refused to let me pass her by as if she didn't even exist. She got into the habit of rubbing against my calves whenever I walked past her and wouldn't quit until I bent down to pet her. The first few times she held me up when I was trying to leave or enter the building, I was irritated. She was a bother, and I was afraid her snaking around my legs would cause me to trip. But then I started noticing that this strange cat's persistence was awakening a kinship in me. Her eyes, pleading for a rub of her black, white and orange coat, reminded me of my age-old need for affection from the people I adored.

I also started to notice the cat's insecurity around her fellows. Her fear was apparent as she flinched when any other stray came near. This strange cat became a kind of mirror for me, reflecting the fear and insecurity I often felt around other people. Sometimes I would be rendered almost speechless when spoken to, yearning to become invisible. The resemblance between this cat and me inspired my mercy.

One day my phone rang. On the line was the owner of the store at the ground floor of my building. He asked me to come downstairs right away to care for a cat that had been run over. When I marvelled at the fact that he called me, of all people, he said he thought this was the cat that had become attached to me. I went downstairs with a heavy heart. At the back of the caller's store lay my friendly stray. From where I was standing, I couldn't identify any injury to her body, but she was lying there as if in shock. Not a limb twitched, and when she looked at me, her green eyes appeared extinguished.

I avoided moving her, fearing that I would make her situation worse. Instead, I just rubbed her head. She didn't react. I summoned my neighbour, Rachel, who had more cat expertise than I, and had been feeding the strays every day for years. After giving the motionless cat a long, concerned look, Rachel went upstairs to get a blanket, then carefully wrapped the limp body and carried the cat over to the building's bomb shelter. She didn't take her into her own home for fear of Felix, her possessive cat. I was worried about Cleo. He was the last cat to join my home, and though he'd been accepted by Jesse, Lady, Mocha and Afro without any objections, I wasn't convinced he'd picked up their knack for hospitality.

Rachel and I decided to keep the cat in the bomb shelter until she recovered, and made a plan for both of us to provide her with food and water. Rachel placed the cat close to the door of the shelter, removed the blanket from her body, then went back home. We remained alone in the dim shelter, the cat and I, for a long time, but she continued to show indifference towards me. I rubbed her head again and spoke sweet nothings to lift her low spirits. Since I found nothing wrong with her body, I decided not to trouble her with a visit to the vet.

Over the next few days, I visited the shelter several times a day in order to relieve the cat's lonesomeness and replenish her food and water supply. Whenever I opened the door I spotted her, curled up in the nearby corner, and each time I was disappointed to find that she hadn't tasted the food I'd left on my previous visit. As I rubbed her head and attempted to entice her to eat out of my palm, she would flee to the back of the shelter.

After three unsuccessful days, when the sorrow in the cat's eyes began to reflect in mine as well, Daphna recommended that I take her to the vet. She said I had to do it, not only for the cat's sake, but for mine as well.

Rachel placed the frightened cat into the carrier I brought from home. Within an hour, the stray was standing on the silver examination table at the vet's clinic. The examination found that her lower jaw was not working, which was why she had refused to eat and drink. The vet fixed her jaw, gave me some medication, and told me not to return the cat to the street until she was fully recovered.

On the way home, I became horrified by the idea of returning the cat to the bomb shelter. In spite of my concern about Cleo's behaviour, I decided to care for the cat in my own home. This was also when I named her – Mishely. I could not yet predict that she and I would be together until the day she died.

Within moments of entering my home, Mishely found herself a hiding place – on the bottom shelf of the kitchen island. The tricoloured cat curled up there, looking at me, encouraged. Perhaps she was trying to thank me for agreeing to house her and tend to her until she regained her strength.

Afro, Mocha, Jesse and Lady showed no interest in our guest. Cleo, on the other hand, seemed flustered. At first he approached the island, curious, wedging his face into the small space of the shelf. Mishely, who'd had little faith in her fellow cats even before her injury, curved her back as if cowering but simultaneously prepared to pounce.

In the course of a single day, Cleo turned from a cat wishing to befriend another to a hostile, aggressive creature. The calmness I'd experienced with my cats over so many years practically vanished when Cleo and Mishely were awake. I had to be on constant alert, ready to stop Cleo from getting too close to the kitchen island. My sleep suffered, too. Every once in a while I was startled awake by the sound of Mishely's terrified yowls, which had me running from the bed to the kitchen. Then I would witness Cleo, standing dangerously close to the kitchen island, gearing up to attack the cat that had rejected him. I didn't know how he would react if I tried to protect Mishely, but I couldn't abandon her to her enemy's whims, either.

At first, I tried to scare Cleo off by raising my voice. I'd yell at him from a safe distance, not wanting him to transfer his rage from Mishely onto me. Then I would beg him to go to a different room. Eventually, Cleo would give in to my distress and abandon the battle I'd averted.

But when Mishely started to recover from her accident, she didn't make do with my protection. Whenever she spotted Cleo approaching her shelf, she would start running all over the apartment, with Cleo in hot pursuit, and me following the two, squealing in an attempt to soothe their fighting spirits.

Ultimately, I started considering returning Mishely to the yard. She appeared completely healthy, apart from her terror of Cleo, which made both of us very nervous. But I also knew I'd have a hard time getting used to her not being around.

My dilemma intensified when Mishely's fear of Cleo began to take a new form. Since she was already feeling at home, and the shelf was becoming too narrow, she would occasionally emerge into the living room, which was adjacent to the kitchen, hop up on the couch, and stretch out leisurely, until Cleo appeared. Then she would stride back to her kitchen hiding spot, though not before leaving a damp spot on the couch or a yellow puddle on the floor.

Shortly before Yom Kippur, I noticed that Mishely kept following me to the door. She would poke her head out and look around the stairwell, then retreat back into the apartment.

Then, on Yom Kippur morning, I was about to go out onto the roof to clean out the litterboxes. As I stood by the door, Mishely joined me, debating, then all of a sudden scampered down the stairs and disappeared.

I was overcome with a joy mixed with sorrow. Mishely's recovery allowed her to regain exclusive control of her life, but also forced me to say goodbye to a life shared under one roof. I didn't know if I'd even see my adopted – or, rather, adopting – cat down in the yard any more. Perhaps Mishely would decide to turn over a new leaf in a different yard, far away.

Throughout Yom Kippur I went down to the yard several times with a false hope of meeting her. Over the next few days, I walked into nearby yards and called out her name. My longing for her grew stronger every day, blending into my concern for her well-being.

A week later, I said a prayer. I prayed for a hint or a sign that Mishely was living and thriving.

Two days went by. At the end of the third day, as I stood outside the building, chatting with one of the neighbours, my thoughts wandered towards Mishely. I looked around, hoping to see her, when all of a sudden she appeared! She ran over and rubbed up against my legs as if we'd never parted. I bent down to pet her, my eyes welling up with happiness and relief. I would never know where she'd spent those days away from me, but it was enough to know that her heart had answered the call of mine, which missed her so badly.

From that evening and until the night before she died, Mishely lived in the stairwell, inside a cardboard box I'd set for her outside my apartment door.

The Soul of an Utter Saint

Every morning, for six years, right after I woke up, I would open the apartment door just to check that Mishely was in her box. Her bright green eyes, looking up into my face, expressed the depth of her love for me with perfect clarity. I also knew how much she'd sacrificed just to maintain our proximity, in spite of the door that remained mostly closed to her.

Mishely was living in forced exile. She had to keep away from Cleo, lest he attack her. My days spent with the two of them led me to conclude that his animosity towards Mishely stemmed from his jealousy of the love that had bloomed between the two of us more than his anger at her rejection of his friendship.

In the morning, when I walked out to see my stairwell dweller, I delivered a bowl of tinned food opened especially for her, then bent down to caress her soft fur. This was a sort of compensation for her giving up the liberty of stray cats, along with her exile from the home behind the closed door.

Some mornings, I walked out into the stair-well but didn't find Mishely there. Each time this happened, my heart skipped a beat; I worried at her absence and was overcome by the void that had replaced her reassuring pres-ence. Since I knew she tended to go down to the yard several times a day, mostly to relieve herself, I would lean over the railing and call out her name. In a matter of seconds, she would stride up the stairs, reporting for duty.

On winter nights, I padded the bottom of her box with a towel and covered her with a blanket. But she seemed to prefer her card-board home to be bare. In the morning, the towel would be shoved into one of the corners. She kicked off the blanket almost immediately.

Beyond the cloud of animosity hanging over Mishely and Cleo's heads, they shared one prominent quality. Unlike my other cats, who did not express a need to be each other's friends, Mishely and Cleo demonstrated a great need for intimacy with Jesse. He acquiesced to their pleas with gestures that expressed his affection for both of them, such as licking Cleo's fur and rubbing noses with Mishely.

Every time I opened the door to the roof, if Mocha, Lady or Afro were out there, Mishely would follow me, the spectrum of her emotions spread out before me. Her eyes were curious; her footsteps hesitant. When she approached most of the cats her eyes were filled with an obvious longing for a gesture of acknowledgement, any sign that they desired her company. But the cats pulled away from her with a reserve that filled both of us with sorrow at her shunning.

On the other hand, when Jesse was on the roof, or when his head poked out into the stairwell, Mishely would become giddy. She got a spring in her step, and her face drew forward with a clear desire to rub noses with him.

One day, Mishely had the pleasure of entertaining a visitor in her cardboard home. A cat who'd lived in the building's yard for many years liked to watch the entry path to the building from a high stone wall. I never felt any special emotion towards her, but her eyes seemed to have caught the trajectory of intimacy that had slowly formed between me and the other yard strays, thanks to Mishely. Perhaps that is what motivated her, one day, to climb the four floors up to my apartment on weary legs and slide into Mishely's box, her feline invasion met with no objections or chagrin.

Mishely's generosity infected me, too, and I started to treat both cats to the special gourmet food. Sometimes I felt bitter over the guest who took over almost the entire space of the box, but I avoided intervening on behalf of the hostess. Still, it wasn't easy to watch Mishely squeezing into the small space left by her friend as they lay in the box together, their bodies flush against each other.

After a few weeks of living as box-mates, the elderly cat's health deteriorated and she stopped going down to the yard to defecate. In response, I placed one of my cats' litterboxes right by the cardboard box.

One day, when the old cat seemed more poorly than ever, my neighbour, Rachel, suggested we have her put down. But that evening, the miserable animal made it down to the yard. That was where Rachel and I found her, hiding underneath a bush, completely exhausted. Rachel placed a box in the bomb shelter, wrapped the extinguished cat with a blanket, and placed her inside the box as if on a deathbed. The euthanasia was scheduled for the following morning.

Rachel called me later that night. Stunned, she begged me to come down to the shelter and behold a magical sight. When I got there, I found both cats inside the old stray's box. The older cat was lying at the bottom of the box, barely conscious. Mishely was lying on top of her, accompanying her pal on her final path, so she didn't have to make the journey in complete solitude.

The next day, Mishely's home was once again hers alone, but she refused to enter it. She persisted in her refusal until I took an action intended to separate life from death, the way Mishely had experienced it the previous day: I went to the grocery store and brought her a new cardboard box. A moment after I switched the boxes, Mishely was already perched inside, her green eyes glimmering with gratitude for my understanding of her need for purification.

The hardships of the body, placed under the incessant threat of the sword of transience, plagued Mishely from the day we came together. I was forced to place her inside her hated carrier and take her to the vet more often than I had any of my other cats. An eye infection that wouldn't go away, a tail that turned as stringy as a shoelace, a loss of appetite that exposed a kidney malfunction and poor circulation. I often wondered at the ridiculing fate that delivered me this test of love, and also tested my finances. While I'd paid good money for all of my house cats, I was given Mishely for free. But in order to provide her with a healthy life, I had to pay much more than I had for the purchase and maintenance of each of my other cats.

Michael, the vet that took care of Mishely from the day I brought her over with the jaw injury that might have caused her death before I had a chance to enjoy our brave friendship, kept claiming that Mishely was imbued with a mental fortitude that helped her overcome the kind of physical failures that would have surely felled almost any other cat. To him, Mishely was a testament to the truth of the notion that cats are born with nine lives. He even said this on the morning of the day that ended with the surrender of Mishely's soul – the day it finally parted from her agonised body.

A few months earlier, I had discovered that every time I stroked Mishely, some fur came off in my hand. The medical diagnosis shook me to my core: Mishely's immune system had collapsed, and her body was attacking itself. She was given medication to slow the onslaught. The only way to get Mishely to swallow the pills was to mix them into food. There was no chance that she would allow me – the way Jesse, Mocha or Lady did – to feed her the medicine while holding her on my lap, making sure it made it into her stomach. This in spite of the fact that Mishely was the only cat who willingly sat on my lap, staying there for as long as I let her.

Every evening, during the time I allocated for both of us to be alone on the roof together, I would sit on a recliner and wait for Mishely to crawl onto my lap so I could rub her fur as she snoozed. I couldn't bear to disrupt her obvious enjoyment of our peaceful union, not even for the purpose of administering medications intended to assist with her body's proper function. I also worried that the smallest interruption to our pleasant time together would motivate Mishely to return to her stairwell abode.

The process of mixing the medicine into her food and monitoring her intake daily to make sure it was emptied filled me with painful tension.

One day, Mishely lost control of her bladder. She also seemed to have trouble walking. Her two hind legs seemed to be hovering above the floor. Her face showed no distress over this newest ailment, but when I saw her limping about on only two steady legs, or staining the area around her box with brownish-yellow puddles, I was filled with pity.

Since I couldn't torture her with another carrier jaunt, I asked Michael to diagnose her over the phone. After every phone call I went to the clinic, bought new medicine, and yearned for a happy outcome. When the urine puddles decreased or even disappeared for a few days, or when Mishely managed to walk on all four feet, I was overjoyed by the knowledge that we'd beaten her disease, or at least managed to put off the symptoms that lurked within her defenceless body.

But ultimately, none of the medications achieved their goal. The urine puddles began to appear more frequently than ever around the box and sometimes even inside it. I had to mop up my landing and the ones below many times a day and procure more and more new boxes that Mishely would agree to enter so she could sleep on a dry surface and gather her strength to continue fighting against her overwhelming sickness.

Finally, I had to admit our bitter defeat. Mishely's body was utterly bony, with scant fur left. Almost every move she made caused her bladder to leak. My cat's suffering became apparent, as if she was ashamed of her body's actions, which were entirely outside of her control. The spark I'd always seen in her eyes was dying.

I knew that nothing would make Mishely happier than being let into my home and becoming a regular tenant. But I also knew I

would never be able to grant her this wish –
because of Cleo, her unrelenting enemy.

Without guessing that Mishely and I were
about to part from her body, which had lost
almost all feline form, one evening I felt I
had to follow my heart's decisive call. That
evening, I was determined to ignore Cleo's
jealousy, which had threatened my bond with
Mishely for years. I lured him into Shlomit's
empty room, locked the door behind him, and
opened the apartment door. In an instant,
Mishely was in my bedroom. As if she were
a spring kitten, she hopped onto my bed and
landed with the ease of a family member right
beside my pillow.

Jesse was on the bed at the time. Mishely
moved closer, leaned her body against his, and
surrendered to the pleasure of this unexpect-
ed, paradisiacal love. I stood at a short distance
from both cats, my heart going out to Mishely
with joy and sorrow. I knew that, in just a few
minutes, I would be the one tasked with ban-
ishing Mishely from heaven. But I took solace
in the fact that I'd allowed her to reunite with
her beloved Jesse, if only for a brief period.
After a few more minutes, during which Jesse

allowed Mishely to lie against him as if she were a part of his body, he stood up and jumped off the bed.

Just then, I heard Cleo's desperate attempts to open Shlomit's door. I urged Mishely off the bed and out into the stairwell, bolstered by the gift I'd granted her in allowing this brief respite on my bed – a seemingly modest gift, but one that, to Mishely, was more precious than any other.

That night, before I went to sleep, I opened the apartment door to check on Mishely. She was lying outside her cardboard house, very close to the door. Her body was like a hunk of meat, petrified with cold. It was pouring outside. As soon as I appeared before her, she looked at me with the kind of profound grief that words could not do justice to. Then, all of a sudden, she got up and strode down the stairs. I followed suit.

By the time I reached the closed building door, Mishely was already there, attempting to push it open with her paw. In spite of the deluge and her weakened health, I opened the door for her. Our love had bound her to me for long enough. As soon as I opened the door, the cat disappeared, swallowed in the torrential rain and the maw of night-time chill.

I left the building door open, and returned home, bawling.

I opened the apartment door over and over again during that sleepless night, yearning to find Mishely on the other side.

She only returned at dawn.

When she had fled into the winter dark, it occurred to me that she might be escaping her imminent death, or, rather, running towards its embrace, preferring to do so in utter solitude. But when I saw her once again outside my door, huddled and wet, I knew she'd made a different choice.

In a split-second decision, I brought the carrier, slipped her inside with no resistance on her part, and carried her over to Shlomit's empty room. This time I locked her inside, rather than Cleo. Wordlessly, I promised her that this room would now be hers. After I'd placed the carrier on the bed and opened it, Mishely crawled out with the remains of her strength, and lay on the soft comforter.

I touched her. Her body was so cold. I placed one towel, then another, over her body, and this time she didn't shake them off. Mishely spent the next few hours in fitful sleep. I lay beside her, softly rubbing her head, wishing for one thing only – for my beloved cat to know, deep under what was left of her fur and her thin skin, that she had finally received the status of permanent dweller in my home. I also decided she would not be leaving Shlomit's room. From time to time, Mishely opened her eyes a crack. When she saw me, she made an effort to lift her head and lick my petting hand.

There was no point in offering her food or water. She didn't even need to swallow medicine any more. My eyes focused mostly on her skinny body. Even in this ugly form, with hardly any fur left, she aroused no disgust in me. Once her body had dried and warmed up, I removed the towels, concerned that they might be too heavy for her. I guessed that if she had the energy, she would have shaken them off herself. Since she was all skin and bones, I could easily see her pulse, which attested to her meek vitality.

*

That evening, after a stressful phone conversation with Michael the vet, who was convinced that Mishely would, once again, wriggle her way out of the jaws of death, I left her in the closed room and drove to Daphna's apartment to get some pet diapers she'd purchased for her recently adopted puppy. I planned to spread one under Mishely's body so it would absorb her urine as she lay on Shlomit's bed. Michael the vet's optimistic forecast imbued me with hope that Mishely would come through.

But it wasn't to be.

When I returned to Mishely's new room, I saw right away that her body was completely still. I was so sorry I hadn't been beside her as she took her final breaths. Then I thought that maybe Mishely, in a final act of loving grace, had chosen to let go of her life precisely when she was left by herself, in order to spare me this most terrible sight.

Three of my cats were buried far away from my home, in an unspecified location. But Mishely – I knew the next day – would remain close to me even in death. I wished to use her eternal

79

resting place as a spot in which to enshrine Shelly, Afro and Lady, as well.

There is a synagogue behind my building, and beside it is a barren patch of land. I knew there was no better place to serve as the eternal home of a saint like Mishely. I asked Yair, the synagogue's superintendent, to give my cat a proper burial.

Yair, a devout cat lover, surprised me. While he dug the grave, he informed me that he used to be an undertaker. Yarmulke atop his head, having skilfully placed Mishely's body, wrapped in one of the blankets I used to cover her on cold nights, at the bottom of the pit, he covered the grave with dirt and stood beside me for several minutes, saying the Kaddish prayer for her soul.

Since then, I visit Mishely's eminent grave every few weeks. Even human saints do not enjoy a burial so close to the house of God. I stand there for a long, peaceful moment, watching the patch of land that separates and unites Mishely and me, and speak words of love, wishing her rest and relaxation that serve as a blessing for me, too.

Sweetheart's Lesson

Dedicated to my yard strays, who strayed to a different yard and never came back

The strays never acknowledged me until I acknowledged them and started to get to know them. We were like neighbours who ignore each other for years, until one day an unusual event forces them to have a single conversation, which gives way to a loving friendship.

Mishely turned me into a friend to the strays, especially those who lived in my building's yard. When she chose the yard over relaxing in the box outside my apartment door, and was late to return to me, I would go downstairs to look for her, and was astounded each time anew by the transformation that occurred in her when she was with the other strays. I was convinced that the new confidence she'd found with them was a result of the love that had blossomed between us.

Following her convalescence in my home, Mishely strutted among the strays like a queen. Rather than flinch when one of them came close, she would act with indifference or hiss them away.

As I watched her, I started observing the other cats, too. At first, whenever one of them noticed my amiable gaze and dared to come closer, Mishely rushed over to cling to my leg in a gesture of ownership. Over time, she became more generous, allowing me to reach out and pet this cat or another. When they became familiar with my touch, some of them even allowed themselves and me to indulge in rubbing the soft fuzz of their stomachs. I knew that, more than anything, permission to touch this hidden part of a cat's body expressed their faith in the goodwill that connected them to a human being.

I started to feed my new friends with the scraps left behind by my cats and their refined palates. Every tin can I opened for Afro, Lady, Mocha, Jesse and Cleo was only partially eaten, and only when it was fresh. After some time had passed, they would no longer touch what was left in the bowls, even if they were hungry. Their eyes would implore me to open a new tin for them. The strays, on the other hand, lunged at the old food, cleaning the bowl out within minutes.

The sight of the strays devouring like starving beggars the scraps I would have otherwise thrown in the bin ignited an intense compassion in me, and this compassion inspired me, whenever I walked out of the building, to bring along a large tin of food intended especially for the strays.

I could never have predicted that this would create a new duty of the heart within me – to come downstairs every day, in all kinds of weather, even when I was despondent or ill, just to feed a growing pack of cats.

Even today, whenever I start to descend the four floors that separate my apartment from the yard, I listen with excitement to the cats chorusing their anticipation of my visit. The same cats that rush off into hiding whenever one of the other tenants or a random visitor walks in or out of the building gather around the front door to welcome me, attempting to open it with their paws so as to hasten my arrival.

Seeing the gaggle of cats pushing against each other, unified in their joy at our imminent reunion, kindles an immense cheerfulness inside me.

I like to speak to the strays while I spend time with them. When they wrestle over a comfortable eating spot, for instance, I scold them in a tender yet assertive voice, like a kindergarten teacher. They seem to understand me, and in spite of their hunger they settle down immediately, taking some space from each other and urging me with their eyes to open the tin, and divide the contents between them.

Over time, I got to know the personality of each individual cat – not needing to define or describe it, judging solely by the level of intimacy and friendliness they expressed towards me. As I became familiar with them, I also developed my preferences. I felt special affinity for the cats whose eyes were full of yearning to be petted. Some cats pushed their hungry faces against my legs, longing for my touch after finishing their meal, or sometimes before I even placed the food before them. A few of them had the honour of being named by me according to the colour of their coat – such as Ginger and Grey – or according to their personality or unique appearance – such as Sweetheart.

A few months after Mishely died, I fell in love with a black-and-white kitten who appeared in the yard one day out of the blue. I named her Sweetheart because of her tiny face, which glowed with graceful innocence, reminding me of a baby.

One day, I noticed a small bulge in her stomach. My neighbour Rachel shocked me when she remarked that the kitten must have been impregnated by an unneutered stray. The sight of the cat's growing gut filled me with pity and I stroked her for a long time.

One day, I spotted her with three white kittens clinging to her. A week later, only one of them was still alive. This kitten's survival forced Sweetheart into early parenthood. The sight of the kitten, his miniscule sleeping body against his mother's, awakened within me a deep admiration for her. Sometimes, the white kitten was alert and energetic, playing with his mother's tail without her having to move an inch. Other times, I watched him suckling from her tiny nipples.

In the first days after the kitten turned into a mother, I stayed away. I didn't want to scare her or interrupt her in playing this part that was completely unsuitable for her young age. But as I dared to come closer and closer, her eyes attested to the fact that she remembered my loving attitude towards her from her pre-motherhood days. She even let me pet her and her tiny son.

When the baby began to muster up the courage to get some distance from his mother and explore the yard's secrets, the young mother was free to roam once more, like a cat dedicated to no life but her own.

Only when the new kitten was a month old did Yael, the vet who had opened a clinic on the ground floor of my building, decide to spay Sweetheart. She explained to me that she had postponed the operation because it would entail separating Sweetheart from her son for many hours, which was too cruel a deed to do while the kitten was still unweaned.

On the day of the operation, Yael called

to inform me that the procedure had been a success, but that Sweetheart had to remain in the clinic overnight for supervision before she could return to the yard and her son. That afternoon, I went to visit her. She was lying drearily in the back of the cage. I asked Yael for a tin of cat food, opened it, took a seat on the floor beside the cage, and opened the door. Sweetheart gave me a melancholy stare, but didn't come near. I started showering her with loving words, until all of a sudden she walked over to me, and took small bites out of the tin. I was filled with joy and relief, just as I was any time one of my house cats began to show the first signs of recovery from illness.

One day, when I opened the apartment door, I was surprised to find Sweetheart's son on the landing, making eyes at me. I immediately re-called the day Cleo showed up on my doorstep. The sweetness of the white kitten enticed me to host him as well, but this time I restrained myself from getting swept up in the special magic kittens hold. I had decided long ago that after Cleo joined his brothers and sisters up in heaven, I would quench my thirst for their company through my friendships with the yard strays. Shlomit and Daphna had grown up and moved out, and it was vital that I focus on my needs alone.

The story of the kitten that was in such need of creature comforts that he ventured up four flights of stairs captivated Yael. She decided to adopt him for her children. I envied her, recalling the days when I was surrounded by five kittens at home. Still, I was comforted by the knowledge that this kitten was redeemed from his life on the street.

His devoted mother, on the other hand, remained homeless. I watched her with curiosity during her first days without her son, looking for any signs of worry or pining for the fruit of her loins that had suddenly disappeared. But just like I did after Daphna and Shlomit moved out, Sweetheart regained the independence she'd enjoyed in her pre-parenting days with no visible difficulty.

One day, Sweetheart disappeared from the yard. She didn't show up the following day, or the day after that. My stomach was in knots.

Whenever I descended the four flights of stairs, I prayed to see her through the building's front door, shoving between her friends to greet me.

Every day brought a new disappointment. More than anything, I was worried about the possibility that she might have been run over and I'd never know. At the same time, I began to wonder if perhaps she'd simply turned her back selfishly on everything I'd given her over the last few months, and moved on to another yard.

A week went by, then two, then three. Occasionally I pondered the things I'd heard often about the nature of cats, which are devoted and loyal mostly to their own ever-changing needs. At the same time, I recalled the bipeds who had captured my heart and then left me high and dry, abandoning their sense of obligation towards me and denying everything I'd given them.

One day, it occurred to me that perhaps Sweetheart was teaching me an important lesson. Perhaps the sudden separation she'd forced upon me would teach me to free myself once and for all from the chains that bound me to loved ones who were long gone. I hoped that if I managed to quickly recover from Sweetheart's disappearance, I'd be released from my fear of abandonment. In the past, I had set aside my own needs and given up my liberty for the sake of new attachments. Each time anew I tried in vain to believe that – as compensation for giving up my selfhood and independence – these people would stay with me for ever.

I'd almost made my peace with Sweetheart's absence from the yard, but then one day I saw her standing on the stone wall that separated my building from the one next door. She just sat there, watching me walking down the path, as if we'd never parted. Her body had filled out; along with the weight, she had gained a robust spirit that she had lacked before her disappearance.

I'll never know where she went off to before she returned to the yard, and I'll never know why she left in the first place. But since then, every time I meet her, I ask myself if I'll be lucky enough to see her again the next day. I keep reminding myself that I ought to focus on all the joy she's brought into my life just by knowing her, and remember that Sweetheart is entitled to determine each day anew the lifestyle that best suits her needs, and her needs only.

What Is Love?

No person has ever loved me like my cats have, and if anyone had claimed to, I wouldn't have believed them. My cats' love for me existed mostly underneath their fur, injected directly under the skin, and often only showed itself through their eyes.

I almost never doubted the intensity of the threads that bound us to each other over approximately two decades and a greater number of hours spent together than I'd shared with anyone else.

Occasionally, when Jesse took advantage of an open door to investigate the stairwell and sprawl out on the doormats outside one of the other apartments, as if waiting for the strange door to open and a neighbour to invite him into a new home, I suspected that he was sick of me. That's what I told him when I stood over him, demanding with angry insults that he return home at once. Then he'd hurry up the stairs behind me, his eyes the very picture of awe and remorse.

I didn't truly view this habit of Jesse's as betrayal. I was mostly upset because it required me to venture downstairs to find out which apartment he'd parked himself outside and beseech him to deign to return to his forever home. This usually happened early in the morning, shortly after I awakened and opened the door to check on Mishely.

In truth, I could totally relate to the cat who seemed to want to defect. I often considered his humdrum routine, spending years and years between the same walls. I knew Jesse was an extremely curious cat, amiable and outgoing. He never hesitated to approach any neighbour who walked past the open apartment door or anyone who visited my home. It was easy to identify the desire in his eyes for a rub of his silky black coat.

And there was the day I locked Cleo in Shlomit's bedroom, giving in to my pity for Mishely, who longed to be let into my home once more. I allowed her to come inside for a short while and even indulged her by letting her sit on the couch. I never imagined that as soon as I let Cleo out of his prison cell, he would attack my ankles with a burning fury, piercing my skin with his sharp teeth. Cleo wouldn't let go of my ankle even after my blood ran onto the floor. I was barely able to release myself from the grip of his tiny jaws. Screaming, I shooed away my attacker and rushed off to the clinic to get an anti-inflammatory shot.

When I returned home with a bandaged ankle, I treated Cleo as I always had, as if there was no bad blood between us. I knew he hadn't hurt me out of animosity, but because of jealousy – I had favoured Mishely and in doing so had threatened his home comforts.

My easy forgiveness also attested to a fulfilment of my deep, long-lived desire to be more like my cats and mimic their ability to quickly shake off the burden of heartrending events. I decided to be more like Cleo, who approached me upon my return from the doctor with an expression devoid of all insult, ingratiation or vengefulness.

*

Of my six cats, Mocha and Lady were the only ones who graced me with the touch of their tongues against my skin. Lady, the white Persian who strutted around on stubby legs – albeit they carried her rotund body swiftly – stuck out a warm, pink tongue to vigorously lick my palm whenever she was near me. She would do this even when I interrupted her from resting in the position that always impressed me – her hind legs spread out before her on the floor, her back against the wall, and her front legs dangling, bent, affording her the appearance of a delicate human.

Mocha, whose flowing brown coat gave him the appearance of a lion, liked to stand behind my head as I lay in bed and fervently lick my forehead and hair. He was the only one of my cats who practically demanded to be stroked. He often shoved his head against my legs, and when I leaned down to pet him, he quickly closed his eyes, a clear hint that he wished for the petting never to end. Sometimes, as soon as I started to stroke him, he would drop to his back and raise his legs up in the air with obvious pleasure.

I typically responded to Mocha's unquestionable need for physical touch, but I often felt that I didn't even come close to satisfying his appetite. From time to time it saddened me to think that perhaps I truly lacked the ability to give enough to my two-legged and four-legged friends. I was constantly preoccupied with compulsive thoughts and emotions, alongside a ceaseless burden of urgent tasks. Sometimes I even got carried away and berated myself, thinking that the great love I possessed for people and cats alike was nothing but fraud and illusion.

Unlike my two-legged loves, my cats almost never meowed any complaints about me. But, like most people I loved, they were the ones who usually dictated the nature of our relationship, including the timing and manner of intimacy and distance between us. Often, just when I desperately needed to have my cats around me – for instance, in moments of upset or lonesomeness – they ignored my pleading, remaining indifferently in their resting places.

I could have got upset or angry, or viewed their aloofness as testament to their selfish characters, but I learned very early on in our relationship that, for cats, there is no direct correlation between affection for people and the compulsion to fulfil their needs or desires. They cater to no one but themselves.

Even when one of my cats answered my pleas, hopped up on my bed and lay down beside me, they would normally depart a short time later, regardless of how pleasant it was to be so physically close.

Clear proof of my cats' concern for my well-being was provided in the mornings. Often, still asleep, I could hear them circling my bed restlessly, as if they feared I would never wake up. Eventually, one of them would cause a commotion by opening the squeaky wardrobe door. Instead of scolding them, I would open my eyes and smile at the alarm cat who now sprawled out on the floor, reassured, and dozed off.

My cats taught me better than anyone else what love is, and how it could be maintained over many years without any need for affirmation through language.

If I ever enjoy such extended, profound

closeness with another person, it would likely happen only when I learn how to live alongside them without giving up my own identity, just like my cats did with me.

A Prince in Disguise

Perhaps as a result of having surrounded myself with five kittens in the course of a single year, with some of them it took months, even years, before I got to know each of their minds. This was the case, for instance, with Jesse, the Persian with the doll face and the glowing green eyes.

I don't remember how old Jesse was when his personality revealed itself to me in full, as if out of the blue. This discovery may have had to do with my sudden realisation that he knew how to speak. His lips would move, but his voice was barely audible. When he looked at me with gaping, expressive eyes, his mouth opened and closed, and from his throat emerged a stifled voice like a person speaking inwardly.

In spite of Jesse's mumbling, I almost always understood what he was trying to tell me.

When he wished to step out onto the roof in the late afternoon, he would stand to attention by the front door, waiting for me to come near. Then he would raise his doll face to me and his mouth would open, as if to say, 'Please, open the door.' Of course I did as he asked.

When I acquiesced to the requests Jesse made with his lips, an approving calm would descend upon him. This happened, for instance, when he asked me to open the fridge and treat him to small chunks of cold cuts. When he wanted to snuggle in bed with Shlomit on her visits from studying abroad, he would stand outside her closed door and wait for me to notice the plea in his eyes and his voicelessly murmuring mouth. Soon after I would open the door for him, he would jump up onto Shlomit's bed and ask her with his eyes to rub the black silk and soft skin of his belly.

A late love blossomed between Jesse and Shlomit. Once it did, she described him as a human being with a captivating personality who took on the appearance of a cat in one of his incarnations. I often imagined that underneath Jesse's black coat dwelled a cursed prince who was lying in wait for the day when he would be liberated from his cat's fur, trading it in for an elegant cloak.

Jesse often appeared beside me just before I got into bed, then followed me in and stood on my stomach. His two front legs would scratch the front of my shirt, his expression lost in pleasure.

Sometimes he would lie on the pillow next to mine and fix me with burning eyes. I often wondered at the concealment of our communication through gazes charged with meanings that could only be interpreted using the language of the body and the heart.

Jesse was an expert at translating his changing desires, which were never many or too indulgent. In fact, he did this with everyone. By opening and closing his mouth, he could articulate, for instance, his desire to inspire affection. He feared no man and no cat, never threatened or attacked, not even out of defensiveness. His face expressed a powerful personality, but not one that was demanding or controlling. When his wishes went unfulfilled, he quickly moved on. For instance, when we hung out on the roof together – with me sprawled on the recliner and Jesse's body splayed between my legs, his head leaning against one of them – he would often open and close his mouth as if begging me not to get up and go back inside. But when I insisted on doing so, he would hop back onto his feet and follow me in, attentive and dedicated to his lady's wishes.

Jesse almost always obeyed my calls to bring me the warmth of his fur and fortify my spirits with his wonderful, enduring intimacy. He presented me with the possibility of pleasing another without the side effect of self-annihilation. Unlike me, Jesse pleased others through a mind devoid of the profound need that drove me – the need to please in order to be loved, especially with the people whose affection was vital to stabilise the ground of my soul, which was restless and shifting most of the time.

It was apparent that Jesse pleased out of a pure desire to indulge people and cats alike. This tendency made him Mishely's only feline friend. He let her rub noses with him whenever they met, a testament to his generous spirit, which always wished to bring joy to others.

A generous love tends to attract a variety of other hearts to it, like a magnet. Perhaps this was why even Cleo exhibited an intense desire to be Jesse's friend. The Siamese that scared off Mocha, Lady and especially Mishely, would roll onto his back whenever Jesse was around. He would put his paws around one of Jesse's legs, asking him to lick his head. Sometimes Cleo was the one who stood over a recumbent Jesse and vigorously licked his beloved's head.

This show of affection between my two cats made me exceedingly happy. That's exactly how I felt whenever Daphna and Shlomit were ensconced in familial bliss, such as when Shlomit played the piano as Daphna stood beside her, singing.

Jesse also stood out among his adopted siblings in his lust for life, which did not diminish a drop in his nineteen years. He was the only one who reached such a ripe age. Even as an old-timer, he retained much of his youthful façade. He continued to roam my home with a lithe and light step. As he grew older, I suspected that this agility was his way of masking the aches and pains of his ageing body.

Just like for my other cats, climbing onto my bed was a kind of physical fitness test for Jesse. Almost till the end of their lives, my bed was my cats' preferred sleeping spot. But how quickly they climbed onto it and the way in which they did so revealed their years, which went by all too quickly.

The effort it took Jesse to get up off the floor was evident. The quick jump that was his signature in his early days was replaced with a grappling move, claws in the mattress, as he pulled his body up. But almost until the day he died, he never gave in to his weakening body. He never gave up.

Jesse's life force was put to an incredibly difficult test in the final year of his life. Just like humans who contract a cruel illness, when Jesse's body was pushed against the wall on the other side of which lurked an awful disease, I sensed the intensity of his will to maintain his famous vitality.

One evening, as we sprawled out on the recliner, Jesse suddenly jumped up as if he'd seen a ghost. He ran around in a frantic panic, then flopped onto his back and kicked his legs up in the air. His eyes widened with terror, and he gasped for air.

A few seconds later, as I leaned over him, stunned, Jesse managed to get back on his feet. His fur, rising and falling fast, attested to his quickened pulse. A few moments later, the exhausted cat lay down again. Only then did I pick him up in my arms and lay him out on my bed, where I petted him, watching him intently, praying for his heart to stop racing as if threatening to break through his skin.

Yael, the vet, who had only opened her clinic in my building a few months earlier, came upstairs, saving Jesse the trip inside the carrier. Her examination discovered a heart murmur, but she claimed that the frightening seizure was a result of a disorder of the nervous system. Like me, she thought we ought to avoid any expensive procedures that would cause Jesse a great deal of distress without any guarantee of an accurate diagnosis. Just as I believed it was better to spare elderly people medical tests or treatments that would be too taxing for their souls, which sought serenity, so I assumed it was best to forego any actions that would burden the elderly cat.

*

Over the next few months, Jesse looked perfectly healthy most of the time. But just as I secretly began to hope the evil spirit had moved on from its victim, it attacked him again. Perhaps this was Jesse's way of signalling to me that my hope for his full recovery was inherently erroneous. He must have known better than me that the seed of illness that had been planted in his body long ago was putting down roots, even if those were mostly invisible.

During one of his seizures, Jesse and I learned that a love of life was not enough to keep out death, especially if the inhabitant of the sick body had already enjoyed a generous allotment of good years. During that seizure, Jesse succeeded in keeping out the envoy of death, but the battle left my cat panting with exhaustion for a long while afterwards.

Yael, who was summoned up to my apartment again, examined Jesse as he hyperventilated. She ordered me to take him to the hospital at once, but I vehemently refused. I knew I was serving as Jesse's spokesperson. Over our many years together, in the few times when I'd forced him into the carrier, he let out a stifled whine that I'd never heard from him at any other moment.

When I asked Yael what else I could do in order to settle Jesse's quickened breathing, she recalled her days as a veterinary intern, when she'd learned the secret of the misleading magic of steroids. They could work miracles in the twilight zone of animal medicine, she said, but without a clear medical diagnosis they could also wreak havoc – even causing a cat's heart to stop.

Though I knew Jesse's heart was weak, I decided to take our chances with steroid treatment, hoping it would save Jesse's life rather than end it.

Once more, I experienced the absolute power I had in deciding my cats' fates for better or worse, even when the benefit of each option was not at all certain.

As if as a reward for my boldness in determining the appropriate treatment for Jesse, the two of us subsequently enjoyed three months without another awful attack. The condition for this grace was that I had to hold Jesse on my lap once a day, ignoring his face as it turned from side to side in refusal, and shove half a steroid pill between his tightly shut lips.

But just as I started to buy into the illusion that I'd managed to extend Jesse's life by a few more years, an event occurred that led to Jesse's death within three days and struck me inconsolable with sorrow.

One morning, Jesse stood by the fridge, demanding cold cuts with the movements of his mouth. But as soon as he attempted to chew on a piece, his jaw twisted and he struggled to swallow. No matter how hard the cat tried to fix it, the wayward jaw was useless to him.

I called Yael right away, but she was on her way to a family vacation. By the time we went to see Michael – our second regular vet – Jesse looked completely healthy.

Michael, who had corrected Mishely's jaw after her car accident, placed Jesse on the examination table and asked his assistant to hold him down as he checked and cleaned the cat's teeth without anaesthesia. When I asked why, he explained that it was too dangerous to put a cat with a weak heart under. He promised me that the treatment was gentle and painless, and the mild-mannered Jesse did not seem to be in any distress.

But after his teeth were cleaned, Jesse had to deal with Michael's famous objection to tangled fur. Throughout my years with cats, I was often accused of neglecting their coats. The truth was, I placed no importance on the appearance of their coats, just as I'd never afforded any significance to my own appearance. When I groomed my cats' fur every few months, I could tell that the brush, with its sharp metal bristles, caused them intense discomfort. In response to the claim that clumpy fur damaged the cats' health and well-being, my cats exhibited no difficulty in being released from the burden of the brush.

Loyal to his belief in the detriment caused by fur clumps, Michael started to shave Jesse – again, without the necessary anaesthesia. He decided to do this even though it had nothing to do with the reason for our visit, and without consulting with me or receiving my permission.

Just like my other cats, who had often suffered under Michael's clippers, leaving the clinic with ugly bald spots, Jesse didn't make a peep during the shaving process, but his growing agony was apparent on his face. Time and again, he tried to release himself from the efficient assistant's paralysing grip.

And what did I do while this was happening? I sat in front of my miserable cat, comforting and promising him that this was for his own good. To disguise my own distress and avoid my feeling of helplessness in the face of Michael's determination, I even chatted with the vet. Even though I felt a recurring urge to whisper to him to stop needlessly torturing my cat, once again – just as I'd done almost twenty years earlier, with Shelly – the awe and respect I had for the medical profession overtook my sense of duty to put an end to my cat's evident agony.

The only encouraging thought I had as I left the clinic was that there was no concerning reason for Jesse's jaw spasm. But what kind of comfort was this in the face of a sight I would never be able to forget? When Jesse was allowed to move freely on the metal table, he couldn't even stand on his own four legs. They splayed out like the legs of a marionette whose puppeteer had dropped its strings. Michael reassured me that this was merely a temporary weakness.

He admitted that the prolonged treatment had caused the patient a great deal of stress and necessitated some time to recover.

My heart went out to the powerless cat. More than anything else, I was filled with a guilt that would never be excused. I had let Jesse be put through this unnecessary suffering, and failed to put a stop to it even when I could have.

When we came home, Jesse struggled to step out of the carrier. He still couldn't stand on his feet. His body, almost bare of its silky black fur, looked utterly gaunt. My bleary eyes witnessed no prince. The cat looked entirely devoid of vitality, and his eyes were fogged. His powerless legs splayed out again, and he remained planted in place beside the carrier I'd just helped him out of.

The hours ticked by. As night descended and Jesse showed no improvement, I looked at him with eyes that cried my grief. I begged with clear – if soundless – words, to God and Jesse as one: if this was my beloved's cat's time to be taken away from me in body, all I asked was that he might be able to stand on his own four feet one final time, to redeem me from an inch of my guilt for abandoning him to such foolish injustice.

All of a sudden, it was as if a miracle took place. Mere moments after I finished voicing my heartbroken prayer, Jesse mustered what little power he had left and stood up. I interpreted his effort as if being made only for my sake and as a result of his immense love for me. He even dragged himself on faltering feet into the litterbox in the bathroom, fought his way inside, relieved himself, then returned to my bedroom, where he fell to the floor, as if fainting.

I recalled the evening when Shelly had begun to recover from the excessive anaesthesia administered during her spaying. I remembered how she'd limped sleepily over to the litterbox. In light of Jesse's difficulty in reaching the box, I was filled once again with admiration for the feline family, which was superior to humankind in so many ways. As long as a cat wasn't at death's door, they would make sure only to defecate where they could hide their eliminations, without troubling anyone else to clean up after them.

*

The next morning, after giving Michael an update, my voice a mixture of terrible anger at him and at myself and desperate tears over Jesse's end, which was speeding towards me faster than I could have ever imagined, I listened once more to his reassurances regarding the temporary stress endured by the sensitive cat. But Jesse's extinguished appearance was, to me, proof positive that cancelled out any artificial human encouragements. If I could only wish for a second miracle, I would turn back time and avoid taking Jesse into the clinic to indulge my own needless anxiety. Had I kept him at home, he would likely not have deteriorated so rapidly.

I knew we only had a few more hours together. There were moments when I wished to see Jesse released as quickly as possible from his suffering body, which had never looked worse. But at the same time, I could sense – as if I myself were Jesse – his familiar thirst for life. I continued to pray for his recovery.

When I called Yael's colleague to my bedroom, I planned to ask her to inject Jesse with more steroids with the hopes of a second redemption.

But a brief look at his bloated stomach as he slept on my pillow was sufficient for the vet to determine drily that the cat was about to die. She recommended that I save both myself and him the agony of death by putting him down.

I wasn't prepared to do that yet. I asked the vet to try to save his life with steroids, as Yael had done three months earlier. When Jesse and I were alone in the room together, I lay on my bed with my stomach against his back, and held him to my bosom. From time to time, he wriggled out of my embrace with great effort, and fixed me with eyes that begged me to quench his thirst. His mouth opened slightly, silently wishing for the miniscule dosage of life that was still available to him.

Jesse and I spent the last night of his life in my bed, in fitful sleep. His furless skin almost blended into mine. I held him close like a baby, mumbling my intense, nineteen-year-old love into his little ear over and over again. I longed for him to hear me, believe me, and forgive me. At the same time, I begged him to let go, to surrender, and to release me of the need to decide the end of his life.

Every so often, I thought I felt the soft, shaved skin stilling its rise and fall. I was washed with a sense of relief mixed with a joy for our release. But then Jesse would lift his head from my arm ever so slightly and beg for some more water.

Jesse, who had never defecated outside of the litterbox, lost all control of his body the next morning. The sheet was covered with urine and faeces. I focused all of my resources on gathering my powers to choose the quickest way out of my cat's terrible misery.

That day, Yael was scheduled to be back at work. I called her and asked her to come upstairs and help me and Jesse part ways. Then I waited restlessly for her to arrive and put an end to the horrid vision of death.

And so we parted – with me seated on my bed, and a gaunt, hairless Jesse lying still and shut-eyed in my arms. Wrapped in one of my oversized shirts, Jesse joined his beloved Mishely that day. When I came home from their adjacent graves by the synagogue, Cleo was waiting. I hugged him and thanked him for allowing me to devote my full attention to

Jesse over the previous two days. The truth was, all of my cats did this when another was sick.

Just like all of my house cats upon the death of one of their siblings, Cleo showed no signs of mourning. But I had no doubt he would miss his friend, even if he refused to disclose the pit that would open up in his soul.

Every once in a while, I asked Cleo if he missed Jesse. If he could have answered, I would have learned another important lesson in cat mourning. But I did not require this lesson. Just like Shelly, Lady, Afro, Mocha and Mishely before him, upon his death Jesse transferred his presence into the depth of my soul, filling it with a living emotion purer and more satiating than any other.

An End Without an End

Saturday afternoon. For fourteen years, we'd spent most of the hours of every day together. In the past year, we were usually the only ones at home.

I'd never before seen Cleo's eyes as they looked that day. Their appearance pulled my attention, startling my heart. A heavy curtain of sorrow draped over them when Cleo looked at me. I tried to ignore the hateful panic I experienced over the years whenever something was amiss with one of my cats.

Cleo was lying on the floor, his little head on the cool metal base of the tall reading lamp in my room. His body was partially hidden by a large armchair. I was lying in bed, calling his name, just as I'd done every day of the past year. When I called him, Cleo would walk over to the bed as if he'd only been waiting for me to summon him. Then he would grip the ends of the colourful bedspread with sharp claws, pull his heavy body up, and cling to me. He almost always succeeded in this climb on the first attempt, but even when he didn't, he never gave up. He would perform a little spin on the rug, gather his strength, and then try again – this time, succeeding.

But not that Saturday. In vain did I keep calling his name, until finally I left my bed, disappointed, and fell straight into the panic his eyes had awakened within me before. I leaned down and rubbed his shorn grey coat. I rubbed and rubbed, waiting to hear and feel his familiar purrs. Only a few came, and they sounded forced as if from a habit that contained no real pleasure.

I walked over to the last litterbox I had left, the one I had placed in the corner of the bathroom once Jesse and Cleo were the only cats in the apartment. I no longer needed the ones that had sat for years in the tiny room adjacent to the roof. In the long era I had spent with my cats, who shared their litterboxes, I could never answer when a vet asked if a sick cat was defecating regularly. But by that Saturday, for months the litterbox had been reserved exclusively for Cleo's eliminations, and it was easy to know how frequently he'd emptied his bladder or his bowels.

The litterbox was perfectly clean. This was an unusual sight. But rather than the anxiety that often plagued me whenever my cats changed their habits, this time I found the clean litterbox reassuring.

In the past few months, Cleo had been suffering digestion problems. I often heard him yowling in the litterbox because of constipation, which I treated every morning by instilling a thick medicinal syrup into his food.

I wondered if Cleo's body was getting too heavy for him, encumbering his motion. I guessed the misery in his eyes originated with an intestinal blockage that would resolve itself promptly. If it didn't take care of itself by the next morning, I decided, I'd call to request some medical intervention.

Cleo hardly budged from the base of the tall reading lamp until Sunday morning. Just as I'd done for all of my cats when they were sick, I brought food and water from the kitchen buffet into the bedroom. On more than one occasion,

I was disappointed when changing the location of the food bowl didn't help, and the expensive delicacy went uneaten in its new spot. The water bowl usually offered a bit of solace. My cats tended to guzzle it down as a sign of their final fight for their spring of vitality.

Cleo had a hard time standing up and sipping from the water bowl I placed under his nose. In an urgent phone call to Yael, I shared the events that had befallen my cat in the previous twenty-four hours, encouraging both of us to believe that his immobility was a result of his clogged intestines. Yael agreed to come up to my apartment to examine Cleo. Secretly, my mind also drew up horrendous memories of my other cats' travails.

Lady had crossed the line between perfect health and complete ill-health in the course of a single day. Her illness drove her to hide in a wardrobe for hours. By the time I noticed and pulled her out of there, she was too weak to stand. For a full week, I fussed around her, insisting on getting her weary body to rest on my bed, softening the blow of her suffering with classical music.

One night, my formidable Persian jumped

up in the middle of the bed, as if suddenly borrowing some of her old life force. Then, less than a minute later, her soul left her body as I held her.

I also remembered how, one morning only a year ago, I'd caught sight of Jesse's mouth twisting up when he tried to eat, and how, rather than delay medical intervention, I'd forced unnecessary treatment on him, from which he never recovered.

My deep familiarity with the minds of all of my cats throughout my years with them had taught me – even if I didn't always follow these lessons – that I had to match my bedside manner to their unique personalities. When Yael arrived, equipped with a stethoscope, she was surprised to find that Cleo's heartbeat was fine. She was also mystified when Cleo didn't move an inch, not even when she held the cold metal against his rolls of fat. In fact, this was the first time she had seen him at all; during her previous visits to my apartment, Cleo had made sure to go into hiding.

Yael and I agreed that she should take Cleo downstairs to her clinic, and Cleo didn't resist when I pushed his body into the carrier, which was much too small for him. When we said goodbye at the door, parting for a brief period of time, at the end of which – I hoped – my cat would be returned to me in fine health, I held on to the idea that my Siamese's intelligence was what led him to allow Yael to do whatever she needed to do in order to heal him. My dilemma regarding the best course of treatment for Cleo would preoccupy me from the moment he descended from the fortress of his home to Yael's clinic on the ground floor.

Thirty minutes later, Yael called me. Agitated, she reported that one of Cleo's lungs had stopped working. Stunned, I asked how it had even occurred to her to do a lung scan. Yael explained that when she'd tried to remove the blockage, he'd gone into severe respiratory distress. She'd taken an X-ray, which had revealed the upsetting finding. Yael instructed me to take Cleo to the animal hospital, where the sophisticated equipment might allow an accurate diagnosis of the reason for his lung failure, and where suitable treatment would be offered.

I refused to take Cleo to the hospital, just as I'd done with Jesse a little under a year before, asking Yael to make do with steroids – they had provided Cleo's beloved with an additional and wonderful three months of life. I flashed back to the last time I'd seen Shelly, in the lobby of the hospital from which she never came home. I felt as if my first cat was crying to me from heaven, summoned once more to her guardian duties.

Earlier, when Yael had examined Cleo in my apartment, I had asked about the sadness in his eyes. She had claimed that only a cat's owner could recognise these expressions, thanks to the intimacy we shared in healthier times. Now, as she pleaded with me over the phone to take the cat to the animal hospital and save his life, I recruited this very argument to support my objection. I was the only one who could say with confidence that Cleo would not make it through a night of hospital examinations, alone and away from me and from the home that had kept him safe and hidden from strangers' eyes his entire life.

Even my famous habit of pleasing my cats' doctors and acceding to their instructions out of a false belief that they would defeat death did not, this time, overcome my stubborn refusal to part from Cleo, not even for a single night.

At the end of the conversation, Yael made an especially grave threat: she warned me that Cleo's shortness of breath could return at any moment. If this happened in the middle of the night when the clinic was closed, she said, Cleo and I might live through a real nightmare. With a trembling voice, she shared her own personal story of watching her father die as he fought for his final breaths.

I begged Yael to inject Cleo with a sedative and asked her to bring him back to me as quickly as possible. In the meantime, I prayed that Cleo wouldn't suffer too much, and that when I felt we were reaching the line of agony and that there was no chance of his regaining his old life – I wouldn't hesitate and find the courage to ask that he be put down.

As I waited for Yael to bring Cleo back up to my apartment, I started wondering if there was any connection between Cleo's sudden deterioration and the coughing fits he'd sporadically suffered from in recent months. During these fits, he would clear his throat for long minutes, after which he behaved as normal.

I had decided to ignore the bothersome

sounds of expectoration. I'd been doing the same for the past few years whenever my own body seemed to be malfunctioning. I remained more faithful than ever to the needs of my soul, and to my ability to endure through discomfort. I was afraid that medical examinations would reveal health problems that would entail extensive treatments and derail the pleasant routine I'd finally fallen into. These treatments might extend my life, but would spoil the peaceful existence I'd wished for over the years.

Cleo returned home and hurried to get out of the carrier and hide between my bed and the wall – his favourite spot. Yael told me that during his time at the clinic, trapped inside a spacious cage, he'd had the opportunity to meet a truly captivating cat. Once he'd been injected with a sedative, he exhibited great interest in everything that took place outside of the cage, watching the cats and dogs that visited the clinic with intense curiosity.

I reported Cleo's coughing to Yael and asked if it might have something to do with his lung collapsing. Yael marvelled at the fact that I hadn't shared this information before, as I had with any other health issue, big or small, that I'd detected in my cats. A fresh bout of guilt assaulted me. This time, I might have stopped Cleo from receiving crucial medical treatment on time.

We both expressed a profound hope that Cleo and I would get through the night without any further breathing difficulties. Yael promised to come back the following day and inject Cleo with more sedative. She also shared her plan to bring a specialist to her clinic for Cleo's diagnosis. The specialist would come equipped with machinery similar to the kind available at the hospital. That way, we might be able to find out what was damaging the cat's lung function.

Wordlessly, I lamented the fact that the specialist could not make the time to come to Yael's clinic sooner. That must be what most people feel in their time of sickness – utter dependence on medical professionals and helplessness at their lack of control of doctors' availability to offer a cure. Then I recalled, with scolding self-rebuke, that I was the one who'd decided not to bring Cleo to the hospital for the very same purpose.

*

That night, I woke up several times to gaze at Cleo as he slept between my bed and the wall. The next morning, before I even got out of bed, I was glad to see him leave the bedroom on his way to the litterbox. A few minutes later, he returned from the bathroom, but rather than jump up on my bed, he plopped down on the base of the reading lamp again.

With great sorrow, I recalled how, only two days earlier, Cleo had looked as if he still had many years to look forward to. Later that morning, Yael would explain to me that cats can often conceal severe medical issues for many months. Then, in one fell swoop, their imagined health deteriorates completely, as if a performance has just ended and the curtain has been lowered.

All day long, I thought about nothing but Cleo. At first I still bothered to open one tin of food after the other. Only two days earlier, Cleo had been eating with gusto. But now the tins were returned to the fridge, untouched. Despair took over when I watched the cat shuffle with effort from one room to the next in an attempt to escape me.

He wouldn't drink water any more, either. That afternoon, he stopped leaving the narrow area between my bed and the wall. He seemed to be having trouble inhaling. Out of a complete mental blindness to his struggle for air, I leaned over him, rubbing his soft belly. He didn't react. I kept showering him with words of love until I finally sobered to the separation that was rushing towards us. From a void of thought and emotion, I broke into tears. I realised that it was only within this absolute inner void that I would be able to find the strength to do what was best for the cat.

That evening, it dawned on me that I had to hurry up and release Cleo from the relics of existence that survived in his body. Sometimes, death dawdles for no reason. On the threshold of my cats' demise, it prescribed the kind of suffering that seemed to have erased the sweetness of all their previous years at once.

The clinic was about to close. Cleo's mouth continued to open with effort, taking shorter and shorter gulps of air. I called and asked Yael to come upstairs with a syringe of euthanasia drug. She praised my decision, which she deemed both brave and wise.

In the time that I waited for Yael to arrive I found a surprising relief. I took comfort in knowing that, in a matter of minutes, Cleo would be released from the imperative to make do with broken breaths that drained all the flavour out of his life. I ran a soft hand through his shorn coat. This hand, whose touch once pleased him so, was now a terrible burden. I gave up, acquiescing to say goodbye without exacerbating his pain. I only hoped that Cleo could hear my words through the thick dimness that already separated us, promising him that redemption was nigh, along with an eternal return to his beloved friend Jesse.

On my first night in twenty years without a cat in my home I found myself concerned about one thing only: I hoped with all my might that Yair, my devoted cat undertaker, would make sure the next morning to dig a new forever home for Cleo right beside the one he'd dug for Jesse the year before.

The next morning, hard as a rock, Cleo lay on the wooden chair that separated Yair and me. The cat was wrapped in the blue towel that had covered the recliner on the roof the day before. Yair was taking pains to push an old, abandoned wardrobe off Jesse's burial plot.

I walked over to touch Cleo's body, which was freezing, having been placed overnight in the clinic's fridge. His face was serene, as if he were in the middle of a deep slumber. The vision that Yair was creating before my eyes ignited my joy, which had been buried by my tears the previous day.

Mishely, her beloved Jesse, and his beloved Cleo, would now be living together, tucked against the back wall of the building. Together, they would form a triangle of friendship and camaraderie. A short distance away – in a manner befitting his isolationist lifestyle – Mocha was lying in his own plot.

Two days went by. On the living-room floor, which had been scrubbed the day before, I found a small, sharp claw. I picked it up and placed it on my desk. Shelly, Afro, Lady, Mocha, Mishely, Jesse and Cleo's concealed yet oh-so familiar souls seemed to have bunched together to form the perfect symbol of love. That was what this claw from my last cat meant to me.

A New Chapter

For weeks after Shelly's death, I didn't dare open the boot of my car and bring home the carrier that had transported her to the animal hospital, from which she never returned. When I finally pulled it out, my eyes fell upon a tuft of fur deep inside the carrier. I held on to the lock of grey hair as if it were a living limb. I have it to this day, wrapped in white tissue, tucked away for safekeeping in the drawer of my bedside table. Alongside it, also packed up in white tissues, are six other locks of fur I cut from the coats of Lady, Mocha, Afro, Mishely, Jesse and Cleo.

Sometimes I am lured to slowly unwrap one of the tissues. I unfold it with my fingers, which long for the furry touch of my tribe of cats. I bring a lock of fur to my lips and kiss it, holding it to my nostrils, imagining that the aroma of cat has remained intact.

There are few chapters in my life that have taken place in such an unexpected manner and which I've read so carefully – a reading that took place mostly between or behind the lines – as this one, in which my cats were the heroes and heroines. Had I not become familiar with the souls of my seven cats – with my own five senses – more familiar than I've ever been with any human soul, I would never have been fortunate enough to know – with my own five senses – my own soul to its fullest extent, and learned to be as kind to it as I am today.

I am the eighth cat in my home, in which I will remain with my seven cats, and perhaps with no other cat but them. But whenever I set foot outside my home, my eyes seek out other cats. I talk to them, feed them, and attempt to buy their trust so that they may let me pet them. Most of the cats I come across must be able to sense right away that I am nothing but a cat in human clothes. This closeness of heart, devoid of all human masks, rekindles my full urge for happiness.

The happiness wick, which would catch fire thanks to my cats' acts of love towards me, performed without having to exchange a single word, is the most precious gift imparted to me by the miraculous opportunity to meet them and love them with an emotion more innocent and pure than any I've ever experienced, before or since.

Acknowledgements

I'd like to offer deep gratitude to my wonderful cats, for the inspiration and the enlightenment you have granted me, which made it possible to commemorate you in this book. To my two beloved daughters, for setting me on my feline journey, which has lit up my soul with incomparable brilliance. To Locus Books in Israel, for falling in love with my manuscript and building a golden bridge for it to walk over. To Serpent's Tail for making my most precious dream come true, giving wings to the purest of loves so that it may cross the borders of language. And to Yardenne Greenspan, who gave the spirit of love, which moves every page in this book, wonderful new words that remain loyal to the original.

Anat Levit
Tel Aviv, 2022